Basic
Chess

hamlyn

Basic
Chess

David Levens

CONTENTS

First published in Great Britain in 2005 by
Hamlyn, a division of Octopus Publishing Group Ltd
2-4 Heron Quays, London E14 4JP

Copyright © Octopus Publishing Group Ltd 2005

ISBN 0 600 60804 2
EAN 9780600608042

A CIP catalogue record for this book is available
from the British Library

Printed and bound in Dubai

10 9 8 7 6 5 4 3 2 1

INTRODUCTION

So you want to play chess? It's one of those games you've always wanted to play but never quite got round to – until now.

Chess is actually quite easy to learn – not much harder than many modern board games. It's learning to play it well that's the difficult bit.

And that's why chess has remained so popular for such a long time – over 1,400 years in fact. No matter how skilled you may become, there is always something new to learn: some new opening idea (these are coming out all the time) or some new technique to master.

The following pages should give you a good grounding in the basic ideas of chess and equip you, after some practice games, to give a reasonable account of yourself. If you become good enough, you may even come up with some opening ideas of your own. But if, after working your way through this book and playing some competitive games, you find the nervous tension of over-the-board play too much, you can always continue to enjoy this marvellous game by post, on the Internet or even against your computer.

Chess has more to offer then just playing the conventional game. There are, and always have been, chess aficionados who preferred to compose problems for others to solve, rather than compete at serious chess. You may simply enjoy solving these. In addition, there are also plenty of chess variations to enjoy: Kriegspiel, swap chess, suicide chess, progressive chess and many others, too. You will find more about these later in this book.

Developed in India around AD 600 from a four-handed dice game called *Chaturanga*, it swiftly spread to Persia and the Arab world, and a few hundred years later it finally arrived in Continental Europe. It did not take long after this for the game to spread into England, Scandinavia, Russia and the western hemisphere. Although Russia has long been the dominant chess power, China,

India and Africa are rapidly catching up. Appealing alike to young and old, male and female, the able-bodied and disabled, all races and creeds, it is now the fastest growing participant game or sport in the world and one of the most popular, with millions of addicts in countries everywhere. And, unlike other sports and games, amateur and professional players regularly compete against each other in tournament and match play.

Chess is a game that will hook you for life. You will be in illustrious company, for countless famous people, past and present, have enjoyed its delights, including politicians, scientists, generals, kings, writers, musicians, artists and sportspeople. Napoleon Bonaparte, for example, was a skilled player and one of his games is included in these pages. The former World Heavyweight boxing champion, Lennox Lewis is equally accomplished, as was the international film star, Humphrey Bogart. who, indeed, was such a fan that he was also a member of the management board of the United States Chess Federation. John Wayne wasn't as accomplished a chess-player as Bogart was, but was good enough to be considered among the top five players in Hollywood. In the world of music there are many keen players, including Madonna, Sting, and the lyricist, Sir Tim Rice (the late John Lennon of the Beatles was also an enthusiastic player).

Steve Davies (six times world snooker champion) has even co-authored a couple of books on the subject and was once the President of the British Chess Federation.

Writers who were hooked on chess include Charles Dickens, Leo Tolstoy, Vladimir Nabokov (who even wrote a novel about chess), Voltaire, Martin Amis and Sir Walter Scott. The popular astronomer, Sir Patrick Moore, is a huge fan, as were the scientist and statesman, Benjamin Franklin and the historian, Henry Buckle.

The surrealist artist, Marcel Duchamp not only designed many chess sets, including a useful pocket one, but was also good enough to play for France. Perhaps the most gifted of all is the professional Norwegian International footballer, Simon Agdestein, who is also a chess Grandmaster.

Chess is a game for everyone; so read on and enjoy.

BEFORE YOU START

Before you begin a game of chess, you will need to know about the individual chess pieces: how to set them up, how each piece moves and their strengths and weaknesses. This chapter will also teach you about winning, drawing and resigning, the special rules and moves that can help you out of a sticky corner and how to record your games.

CHESS SETS

A chess set consists of 16 white men and 16 black men, each with 8 pieces and 8 pawns. Chess sets come in many different guises, including fancy sets of men representing famous characters from literature. However, competitive chess is now only played with chessmen of the Staunton pattern.

STAUNTON CHESS SETS

Staunton was a famous English master, who many considered to be the greatest player in the world in the early part of the nineteenth century. He designed the pieces that to this day bear his name. Staunton-pattern sets are sold by most good sports stores or by mail order from a specialist chess supplier. They are usually made of boxwood or plastic and are relatively inexpensive, although more expensive sets with weighted and felted pieces are also available.

TYPES OF BOARD

Like chess sets, types of board vary. They can be made of folding board, vinyl (which can be rolled up when not in use) and wood, with the last being the most expensive. Most of the cheaper boards have the letters a–h printed along the top and bottom, and the numbers

1–8, printed down the sides. You may find this helpful when you first start, particularly in understanding chess notation (see page 11).

THE GAME

Chess is in essence a game of war that takes place between two armies on a square battleground divided up into 64 black and white squares. The main aim of chess is not to annihilate your entire opponent's army but simply to capture (checkmate) his or her King. It is this that gives chess its subtlety and complexity.

There are many ways of checkmating, some simple and some complex. We shall explore various checkmate patterns and how to engineer them later in this book.

YOU AND YOUR ARMY

In a sense you are the general of your own army and it is your skill that will ultimately determine the course of the battle. By being aggressive early on you may achieve a rapid victory, although this is most likely while you and your opponent are still at the novice stage. Later on, when you know the game better, you will learn how to defend your pieces against aggressive moves. As you improve, you will find that your games may take longer, and it may well become necessary to eliminate much of your opponent's army before you can get at the King.

CHESS NOTATION

Almost since chess began, we've been able to have action replays of famous, and not so famous, games. Of course we cannot actually watch the many great players of centuries past in action, but we can play their games over and over again. This is achieved by the means of chess notation.

Chess notation is a form of code used to indicate the moves played. Over the centuries it has slowly evolved, and today almost everyone uses the internationally accepted system that is known as algebraic notation. In this system every square is given a reference consisting of a letter and a number. Starting from White's side of the board, the first horizontal row (rank) of squares are all numbered **1**; the second rank

2, and so on. Looking up the board the left-hand column (file) is designated **a**; the file to the right of this is **b**, and so on. Thus the bottom left-hand corner square is **a1**, the square on its right **b1**, the next **c1**, until we reach the right-hand square **h1**. (See diagram 1.)

In competition chess, where chess clocks are used, chess notation is essential to record and thereby ensure that the correct number of moves are played in the given time.

RECOGNIZING THE PIECES

The pieces are quite easy to recognize. The Queen is topped by a recognizable crown; the King has a crown topped by a cross; the Bishop is shaped like a bishop's mitre; the Rook (Castle) looks exactly like a castle; and the Knight is fashioned in the shape of a horse's head. The top of a pawn is roughly in the shape of a medieval soldier's hat.

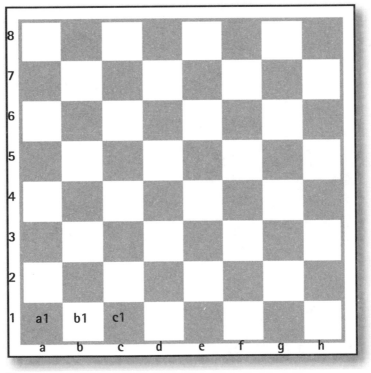

Diagram 1

SETTING UP THE BOARD

Place your board in front of you with a white square in the right-hand corner. If you are White this should be h1 (see diagram 2). Place one white Rook (Castle) on this square and the other white Rook on the bottom left-hand corner (a1). Repeat this process with the black Rooks, placing them on a8 and h8. Now place the white Knights next to the white Rooks on b1 and g1 and repeat for the black Knights, placing them on g8 and b8.

Moving farther towards the middle, place the appropriate Bishops next to the Knights. The white Queen is then placed on the central white square on the first row (each row is called a rank) and the white King is placed on the central black square on the first row – d1 and e1 respectively. The black Queen goes on the square d8 and the black King goes on e8. The white Queen always starts the game on a white square and the black Queen on a black square.

Once you have set up your men as shown in diagram 2 you are ready to start.

THE TOUCH–MOVE RULE

An important rule of chess is that a piece must be moved once you touch it. Leaving your finger on the piece while you decide where you finally want to place it is not unusual in beginners, but is not usually seen in serious play. Experienced players simply work out their moves in their head, then move the piece or pawn to the appropriate square and release their grip immediately. If you wish simply to adjust a piece on its square without being obliged to move it, then say out loud, 'j'adoube' or 'I adjust' before you touch it.

WINNING THE GAME: CHECKMATE AND RESIGNING

In your early friendly games it is likely that you or your opponent will be checkmated, but this is much more rare in serious chess. In competitive games, when one or the other side sees that a position is hopeless, he or she is more likely to surrender (resign), which is done by laying down the King. So, although decimating your opponent's army is not the main aim of the game it can help achieve victory. Games may also be won when your opponent is unable to complete his or her moves in the allotted time. (See 'Chess Clocks' on page 24.)

DRAWING THE GAME

A game can also be concluded as a draw. This can occur through stalemate, perpetual check, repetition of the exact position three times during the game, no pawn or piece being taken for fifty moves or both players agreeing to a draw by shaking hands on it. We will explore these in more depth later.

Diagram 2

NOTATION SYMBOLS

The pieces are each assigned a capital letter:

KING	= K
QUEEN	= Q
ROOK (CASTLE)	= R
BISHOP	= B
KNIGHT	= N

PAWNS have no letter assigned to them

A PIECE-BY-PIECE GUIDE TO THE MOVES

KING

The King can move in any direction, horizontally, vertically or diagonally, but by only one square at a time. Any opposing piece standing next to the King, but not defended by one of its own army, can be captured by the King. Opposing Kings cannot stand on adjacent squares.

In diagram 3 the black King may move to d4 or capture the white Knight on d6, but cannot move to d5 as it would put itself in check. It can move to e6 and capture the white pawn, or move backwards to f4 and capture the white Rook, but cannot move to f6, where it will be in check from the Rook on f4, or to f5, where it will be in check from the Rook on f4 and the Bishop on e4.

QUEEN

The Queen can also move in any direction, but can move as far as she likes along the same straight line, providing of course that no other piece, black or white, impedes her movement (the Queen cannot jump over other pieces). When the Queen reaches the square she wishes to occupy she can capture any opposing piece standing on that square, whether that piece is defended or not. However it is worth bearing in mind that the Queen is worth roughly twice as much as a Rook, three times as much as a Knight or Bishop, and nine times as much as a pawn (see pages 17–21).

In diagram 4 the white Queen can capture the black Knight on h1, or the black pawn on h4, or the black Rook on a5, or the black Bishop on e6, when it will give check to the black King.

Diagram 3

Diagram 4

Diagram 5

Diagram 6

Diagram 7

ROOK

Like the Queen the Rook is only limited in its movement by the edges of the board but, unlike the Queen, it can move only vertically or horizontally, not diagonally. The Rook captures the enemy by landing on a square occupied by en enemy piece. See diagram 5

BISHOP

Bishops move along diagonal lines only, up to seven squares at a time, forwards or backwards. Bishops capture enemy pieces the same way as all other pieces.

In diagram 6 both black Bishops are on their longest and most useful diagonals. The black-squared Bishop on a1 may move right to h8 and capture the opposing Queen on that square or the player of the black pieces may decide just to play it to e5 for instance. The white-squared black Bishop may travel anywhere along the diagonal from a2 (where it will capture the white pawn) to f7 (where it will capture the Rook), anywhere from h1 to a8 or may be played to e6 where it will give check to the white King standing on c8 and from where it will also fork (see page 36) the Knight on f5 and the Rook on f7. Once the white King has moved out of check the Bishop will then be able to capture either the Rook on f7 or the Knight on f5, but not the Knight on g4.

KNIGHT

The knight is the only piece that can jump over other pieces; it is not impeded by friend or foe standing in its way. The knight moves two squares forward or backwards plus one square sideways, or two squares sideways followed by one square forward or backwards: an L-shaped manoeuvre. Knights capture enemy pieces in the same manner as other pieces.

In diagram 7 White has opened 1.Nf3 and Black has replied 1...Nf6. Knights are the only pieces that can move before a pawn has been moved.

In diagram 8 the Knight on the square d5 attacks the following eight squares: c7, b6, b4, c3, e3, f4, f6 and e7. This is a multiple fork (attacking King, Queen and Rook is called a family fork); the black King is in check and, after the King has moved out of check, the Knight may capture the Rook on b6, the Queen on e7 or the pawn on f6, or the Bishop on c3, yet the Knight itself is not under attack from any of the enemy! This is one of the Knight's great strengths – it can attack other pieces and pawns, without any of them being able to return fire at the same time.

Diagram 8

PAWN

The pawn is the lowliest man in either army; it is the only man that cannot move backwards. Pawns move forward just one square at a time, though on their first move only they may be moved forward two squares. Pawns capture by moving one square diagonally to either side and removing the enemy pawn or piece standing on that square. In diagram 9 White has just played his pawn from f2 to f4 giving check to the black King on g5 and, at the same time, attacking the black Knight on e5 (a pawn fork – see page 36). When the black King moves out of check, the pawn will be able to capture the Knight on e5. The pawn on g3 has already moved one square (g2–g3), while the pawn on e2 still retains the option of moving one square or two for its first move, once the black Rook moves out of its way.

Diagram 9

If a pawn manages to fight its way through to the last row of the board (designated the eighth rank) it is exchanged for another piece. In diagram 10 White is about to play his pawn from c7 to c8 promoting it to a Queen, Rook, Bishop or Knight, but never another King.

Diagram 10

Diagram 11

Diagram 12

Diagram 13

SPECIAL MOVES

CASTLING

This move allows you to place your king into relative safety. From its starting square, the King is moved either two squares to the left or two squares to the right, and the rook is moved over the King and placed on the adjacent square. This move is only possible under the following conditions: neither the Rook nor the King must have moved from their starting squares at any time in the game; the King must not be in check (threatened by an enemy piece) nor must it move across, or on to, a square attacked by an enemy piece; there must be no pieces between the Rook and King at the start of this manoeuvre.

In diagram 11 the black King may not castle on either side because the King has moved. Note that moving the King back to its start square, in this case e8, would change nothing – the fact is that the King has moved.

The white King can castle on the Kingside (shown as 0–0 in algebraic notation) by moving the King to g1 and the Rook from h1 to f1. (See diagram 12.)

However White cannot castle on the Queenside (shown as 0–0–0 in algebraic notation) because the King would not only move through the square where he would be in check (d1), but when he arrived on c1 he would be in check there too.

EN PASSANT

En passant (French for 'in passing') is a rather unusual manoeuvre that can be carried out only by pawns. When a pawn, on its opening move, moves two squares and then arrives on a square adjacent to an enemy pawn, the enemy pawn may capture as if the first pawn has only moved one square. However, this capture cannot be delayed; the en passant capture must be made immediately, if it is to be made at all. (See diagram 13.)

In the above position White has just played a pawn from e2 to e4, attacking Black's Bishop on d5. Black can now capture en passant by moving his own pawn to e3, as if White had only moved his pawn one square. Note that if White had been playing from e3 to e4 instead, en passant would not be possible.

THE STRENGTHS AND WEAKNESSES OF EACH PIECE

PAWN
(nominal value 1 point)

Strictly speaking the pawns are not pieces. All of the figures in a chess set are called *men* and are divided into *pieces* (King, Queen, Rook (or Castle), Knight and Bishop) and pawns.

Your pawns are the humblest unit in your army and their biggest weakness lies in the simple fact that they cannot ever move backwards. In practical terms this means that you must take great care in how you

COMPARATIVE VALUES OF THE CHESS PIECES

PAWN	= 1
KNIGHT	= 3
BISHOP	= 3
ROOK	= 5
QUEEN	= 9
KING	= 0

move them: once you have advanced this lowly foot soldier he cannot retreat!

In diagram 14 Black has just played his pawn from d7–d5. This has left his pawn on c6 backward (none of its fellow pawns behind it on an adjacent file) and on a half-open file. (See glossary, page 187.)

If White plays his Rook to c2 to attack this pawn, Black will be forced to play his Rook to c8 to defend it – the pawn that has been moved to d5 cannot return to d7. Because of this the pawn on c6 will soon be lost; White has only to move his King to e5 and then to d6 and the capture will be complete. Also in this diagram Black's pawns on g6 and g7 are doubled and therefore not so easily mobilized as White's pawns on the same side of the board.

The famous master, Philidor, once said, 'pawns are the soul of chess'. This is a saying that has stood the test of time. The whole game may depend on the quality of your pawn structure (your battle formation).

Diagram 14

Diagram 15

Diagram 16

Diagram 17

KNIGHT
(nominal value 3 points)

The Knight is considered a minor piece, but it alone can jump over other pieces and pawns – nothing gets in its way. It is a superb defender, being able to cover several points of attack from different directions at once. In diagram 15 the lone black Knight is preventing the powerful white Queen checking the black King on any of the four squares: c4, c6, g4 or g6.

The Knight is the best blockader of an opponent's isolated or passed pawns and is the ideal piece to place on an outpost square. In diagram 16, if Black played too casually by moving his Rook on d8 to g8, White could play say Nb5 – attacking the black Queen on c7 – and then hop in to d6 – an outpost from which it could not easily be removed by Black, and from where it would attack several squares in Black's position. A Knight has an extremely strong advantage in that it is able to attack up to seven of your opponent's pieces at once, as well as the square it has just left.

The Knight is also an excellent piece in a blocked position, where it can often prove superior to a Bishop. In diagram 17 the black Bishop is hemmed in by its own pawns, most of which are on the same colour squares as the Bishop, preventing its easy movement around the board. In such a position White's Knight is far more mobile and can easily outmanoeuvre the Bishop.

A Knight and Queen working together make possibly the deadliest attacking combination on the board as the Knight can attack different-coloured squares at will, making the defender's task particularly difficult, and the Queen can move in any direction.

So what is the weakness of this paragon of the chessboard? The Knight's main limitations are that it simply cannot cover ground quickly enough, nor attack the enemy without getting in close, nor pin (see pages 34–35) or skewer (see pages 36–37) another piece. On an open, uncluttered battlefield the long-range power of the Bishop may prove superior. This weakness of the Knight is particularly noticeable in a pawn race in an endgame.

In diagram 18, Black, recognizing how far away the white Knight is from his pawns on b4 and a4, has just engineered, or forced, an exchange of pieces on f2.

Now, by playing his pawn from b4 to b3, Black can force a win. If White tries to ignore the pawn by playing a3, Black simply moves his pawn forward another square to b2 and the white Knight cannot get back in time to prevent Black promoting. If, instead, White captures the black pawn, axb3, then Black plays his other pawn to a3 and will promote on a1. Once again the white Knight cannot return across the board quickly enough to prevent Black gaining a new Queen. It is worth pointing out that if the piece on g5 were a Bishop rather than a Knight, all White would have to do would be to play Bf6 and the black pawns could easily be stopped.

BISHOP
(nominal value 3 points)

The Bishop, another minor piece, is a long-range piece, able to move quickly from one side of the board to the other and to attack the opposition from far off – a wonderful attacking or defensive piece in an open position.

The position in diagram 19 gives an excellent example of the Bishop's dual powers. Here both black Bishops defend the important squares around their King, especially f7, g7, g8 and h8, while contributing to a dangerous attack on the white King.

Master players consider the Bishop such an important minor piece that they are reluctant to exchange it for an opponent's Knight. To make this exchange willingly they need to gain some extra compensation, such as doubled pawns. (See Glossary, page 186.)

Black exchanges his black-squared Bishop for White's Knight, which was standing on c3. This doubles White's pawns on c3 and c2, so that they can no longer protect each other. Black also gains other compensation for giving up his Bishop for White's Knight: he can now open up the c-file whenever he

Diagram 18

Diagram 19

wishes and use his Rooks to attack down this avenue. (See diagram 20.)

While the strength of the Bishop lies in its long-range attacking abilities, this same strength can be used against it: in a closed, cluttered position the Bishop can often be no more use than a tank in the middle of a forest! Also a Bishop is truly colour prejudiced. Each Bishop can only attack pawns or pieces on its own colour squares. A Bishop that is placed on a black squares can only attack the enemy on black squares – pawns or pieces on white squares are under no threat from it! For this reason a pair of Bishops, one covering the white squares and the other the black squares, are worth rather more than the sum of their two parts.

ROOK
(nominal value 5 points)

The Rook, like the Queen, is a major piece. Like the Bishop the Rook is also a long-range piece, but unlike the Bishop the Rook is not confined to squares of one colour. It can control a whole line (a rank or a file) single-handedly. By simply occupying the seventh rank (see diagram 21) the Rook can confine

the opponent's King to the back rank and prevent it taking any part in the endgame.

In the position shown, the white King is trapped on the first rank and cannot help its Rook to force home the pawn on a4. On the other hand the black King can move freely and will soon help its own Rook to round up White's pawn.

By controlling a file the Rook can penetrate right into the heart of the opposition camp. And whereas two Bishops or a Bishop and a Knight need the assistance of their King to help checkmate a lone King, a pair of Rooks can mate the opposing King without any other help (see check, pages 28–30 and checkmate, pages 30–32). Even the mighty Queen needs at least the aid of its own King to deliver mate.

The main weakness of the Rook is similar to that of the Bishop: it needs room to operate effectively. Also the Rook plays little more than a passive role until the opening phase is over.

QUEEN
(nominal value 9 points)

The Queen, with its ability to move in any direction you want and attack the opposing

Diagram 20

Diagram 21

army from long range, is easily the most powerful piece on the board.

Diagram 22 gives some idea of the Queen's power. Though Black has a Knight less (in other words, is a Knight down) the white King is in a precarious position and only the Rook on g1 prevents Black from delivering checkmate.

Black now plays his Rook to e1! If White captures the invading Rook with his own Queen, Black can play his Queen laterally along the fifth rank to h5 to reach checkmate! If, instead, White captures the Rook with his own Rook, Black moves his Queen, this time along the diagonal, to g2, checkmate! Thirdly if White tries to avoid both of these captures, by moving his Queen out to g4, Black simply sacrifices his Queen (Qh1+) and, after white takes the impudent Queen (Rxg1), Black takes the Rook on h1# (checkmate).

This strength of the Queen – its ability to move rapidly to almost any square on the board – can sometimes lead to its downfall: if it moves out on to the battlefield too early, especially into the opponent's half of the board, it can easily be trapped and lost. The Queen is a poor defender.

KING

Although in many ways the King is the weakest piece on the board, it is also the most important. It is impossible to put a value on this special piece – quite simply, it is beyond price. Without a King on the board a proper game of chess cannot be played.

From the early stages right into the late middlegame, your King needs to be carefully protected. However, as you enter the phase of the game known as the endgame, when it becomes more difficult to checkmate easily, the King plays an important part in the proceedings. It can now enter the fray with vigour, attacking and capturing enemy pawns and helping to shepherd your own to the eighth rank and promotion. It can also play an important part in mating the opposition King. In diagram 23 Black has a material superiority (two extra pawns) but White, by playing his King to g3, prevents his opposite number escaping a deadly mating net. This advance of the white King now threatens Rook to e5#, and if Black defends by playing his Knight to d4, White can now play his pawn from h2 to h4+. Black then has to reply, Kh5, when White ends the game by playing Rook takes h7#.

Diagram 22

Diagram 23

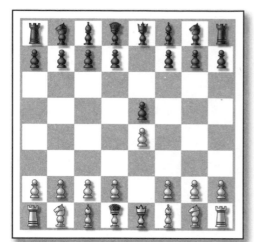

Diagram 24

Diagram 25

Diagram 26

COMMON SYMBOLS USED

There are a few other symbols that you need to know to understand a published game.

x	= captures
!	= good move
!!	= excellent move
?	= poor move
??	= blunder
?!	= a questionable or risky move

RECORDING A GAME

It is time now to put together what we have learned so far and show how a complete game is recorded. Imagine you are playing as White. Start by moving the pawn in front of your King two squares (pawn to the square e4). To record this, simply write e4. If your opponent now replies in kind and opposes your pawn with his own, by playing his pawn from e7 to e5, you write e5. Your score sheet should now look like this.

White	Black
1.e4	e5

And the position should look like this (See diagram 24.)

Now White may play his Knight on g1 to the square, f3, attacking Black's pawn on e5. Black defends by moving his Knight from its start square, b8, to c6. These moves will be:

2.Nf3	Nc6 ... and the position will

now look like this (See diagram 25.)

The next few moves could be ...

3.Bc4	Bc5
4.c3	Nf6
5.d4	exd4

Diagram 27

Diagram 28

6.cxd4 If you have been following correctly, the position should now look the same as in diagram 26

Black now moves his Bishop to b4, checking White's King. This you record as **6...Bb4+**. White defends the check by playing his Knight to c3, so the sheet should now show this:

6...   Bb4+
7.Nc3 As White's Knight, the one on c3, is now pinned by the black Bishop (that is, it cannot move without putting its own King in check), Black can safely capture the white pawn on e4 with his Knight.
7...   Nxe4 White decides to seek safety for his King through castling (0–0).

8.0–0	**Bxc3**
9.d5	**Ne5**
10.bxc3	**Nxc4**
11.Qd4	**Ncd6** The Knight on square c4,

as opposed to the one on e4, moves to d6.

12.Qxg7	**Qf6**
13.Qxf6	**Nxf6**
14.Re1+	**Kf8**
15.Bh6+	**Kg8**
16.Re5	**Nde5**

17.Nd2	**d6**
18.Nxe4	**dxe5**
19.Nxf6# (checkmate)	

If you have managed to follow this notation correctly, the final position should be exactly as in diagram 27.

This little exercise has covered most of the notation necessary to record and follow a game. The three moves missed out are Queenside castling (see page 16) and capturing en passant (see pages 16–17) and double check.

Capturing 'en passant' is recorded in exactly the same way as an ordinary pawn capture. Referring to diagram 12 in the section on chess moves (see page 16), if the black pawn on d4 captures the white pawn on e4 en passant, you record this as dxe3.

Double check is a situation we have not encountered yet. It is depicted as ++, see diagram 28 for an example of this.

In this position White can move his Bishop to either c6 or g6, giving check to the black King. However, at the same time, White will also 'discover' a check with his Queen on e1. As the black King will now be in check twice at the same time this is referred to as double check and is recorded as Bg6++.

CHESS CLOCKS

The image that chess has of being a slow game is almost certainly a hangover from the late nineteenth century. Up to then there was no limit on how long a player could take over his moves and it was quite common for some to spend two hours or more over a single move! Hourglasses were introduced in 1862, with the stipulation that each player should make 24 moves in two hours, an average for each player of five minutes per move. Chess clocks were introduced in 1883.

A chess clock is two normal clocks housed side by side in a single unit and linked, so that, at the press of a button one is stopped and the other started. Thus each player's moves are timed independently of the other. Today, at the highest level of tournament play, the time limits are currently around 40 moves in two hours for each player, so each player has an average of three minutes per move. In league chess, time limits vary from league to league and country to country, but generally average out at just over two minutes per move.

Analogue clocks have been used for many years but are slowly being replaced by electronic versions, particularly in international competitions. With analogue clocks a red 'flag' is pushed upwards by the hour hand from about three minutes to the hour, falling back down on the hour precisely. If this falls before the required number of moves has been completed, the player concerned is deemed to have lost. There is, however, an exception to this: if you checkmate your opponent on the very last move before time control but before you have time to stop your clock. If this happens, then you are still deemed to have won. This ruling was brought about after an exciting climax to a match in the London Boys Championship in the late 1950s, when Dave Rumens checkmated Dave Mabbs, only for

his 'flag' to fall before he could stop his clock. The final result of this game, on which the result of the Championship depended, could not be decided until the International Federation (FIDE) met later that year.

Electronic clocks, which are more commonly used today, have several advantages over analogue clocks. The main advantage is that both players can clearly see, down to the last second, the amount of time left. which is less clear on analogue clocks. Time scrambles, where both players have only a short amount of time left to complete all their moves, can be enormously exciting to watch. I have seen a player make 17 moves in just one and a half minutes, and have myself had to complete 23 moves in six minutes. Unfortunately the media rarely pick up on this exciting aspect of serious chess – it would certainly dispel the myth of chess as being a slow game.

A bonus of chess clocks is that they have made all sorts of fun games possible. The two most popular of these are Rapidplay (sometimes known as Game 30) and Blitz (Game 5). In Rapidplay each player has just 30 minutes in which to complete all his or her moves, so the total length of the game can be no more than one hour. In Blitz both players normally have only five minutes each in which to complete all their moves. Another form of quick chess is Lightning Chess. In this heart-stopping version an electronic buzzer or some other form of sounder is used, set to go off every ten seconds. The player whose turn it is, must move on the buzzer. For the first ten or twelve moves play can seem awfully slow (in traditional chess opening moves frequently being played fairly swiftly) but after that it is all too easy to make serious errors. The great thing about such games is that they are great levellers, even strong players often committing appalling howlers under the pressure of time.

CHESS
TACTICS

Chess is a game of tactics and in order to learn how to play, you will need to be familiar with the principles that guide the main tactics. In this chapter you will learn how to give check and checkmate and how to recognize the common mating patterns. Examples of basic tactics, such as pins, forks, skewers and back-rank weakness are also given to help you beat your opponent.

CHECK

The cry of 'check!' is simply a way of warning your opponent that his King is under direct attack from an enemy piece. While it is always worth considering a possible check, my advice would be to only play it if it gives you some advantage.

USING PAWNS TO GIVE CHECK

In diagram 29 White has just played his pawn to g6, giving check. In other words, the pawn on this square is attacking the black King. Black MUST stop the check, and can do so either by capturing the pawn (hxg6) or moving the King to g7 – a square that is not under attack. Because pawns can only give check when they are one square diagonally in front of the enemy King, check cannot be stopped by interposing another of your men.

USING THE KNIGHT TO GIVE CHECK

In diagram 30, a position you will soon come to recognize (see Common opening traps, pages 98–109) the black King has just moved to d7 to prevent White playing Nc7+, which would fork the King and the Rook standing on a8. White now plays, **Nxe5+**.

As with the pawn, it is impossible to block a Knight check by interposing a piece or a pawn. Either the attacked King has to move to another square or the attacking Knight must be captured. If you examine the position given, you will realize that Black has no option but to retreat his King to e8. It cannot go to either c7 or d6, because both of those squares are already attacked by the Knight on b5. Nor can it move to c6, because this square is now attacked by the Knight giving check; and it cannot move to e6, because this square is attacked by the Bishop on c4. Once the black King has retreated to e8, White can give another check, Nc7, and this time the black King cannot find a square that is free from attack; therefore, checkmate (#).

USING THE BISHOP TO GIVE CHECK

In diagram 31, Black can now play his Bishop from f8 to b4 and give check. From here White has several options: he can simply move his King to a white square, f1 or e2; or he can interpose either Knight, Nfd2, Nbd2, Nc3, c3, or even Qd2?? – although this last move would mean giving up nine points to gain three. Also, if White had a pawn on a3, he could capture the checking Bishop. One thing White cannot do is castle out of check: the rules do not allow this at any time.

USING THE ROOK TO GIVE CHECK

Diagram 32 gives an example of Rook checks. The white Rook on a2 is giving check to the black King standing on g2. As you can see, Rooks, like Bishops and Queens, can give check from a long way off. Once again the black King has several ways of getting out of check. He could remove the offending Rook by playing Bxa2, although White could now recapture with his other Rook, the one on a6, and give check again. Black could also play his pawn to f2, blocking the check by the Rook, or he could move his King to another square (f1, g1, g3, h1 or h3). His final option would be to play his Bishop to e2, not only blocking the check by the white Rook, but also giving check himself to the white King positioned on d1.

Diagram 30

Diagram 31

Diagram 29

Diagram 32

Diagram 33

USING THE QUEEN TO GIVE CHECK

In diagram 33 Black has just captured the white Queen, giving check to the white King on e1. Once again White has various ways of getting out of check. He can move his King off the e1–a5 diagonal – to f1, e2 or d1 – or he can play either of the two Knights or the pawn on c2 to c3, blocking the check. Other possibilities are to block the check by playing Bd2 or capture the black Queen by playing Nxb4, removing the checking piece altogether. (Don't forget that Knights, like all of the other pieces, with the exception of the pawns, can also move backwards as well as forwards).

GIVING CHECK THROUGH CASTLING

Finally it is also possible to give check by castling, such that in the castled position your Rook opposes the enemy King on the same file, either f1 or d1, depending on whether you have played 0–0 or 0–0–0.

Here, in diagram 34, it is White to move. He can either play a3, to prevent the black Rook capturing the pawn on a2, or instead play 0–0+, and then move his Rook to a1, defending his a2 pawn.

Diagram 34

CHECKMATE

To be able to announce 'checkmate!' you must have your opponent's King in check and in such a position that whatever move he makes he will remain in check.

FOOL'S MATE

The simplest of all checkmates is called 'Fool's Mate' (see diagram 35), as the game is over in just two moves. Such a checkmate occurs rarely, because it depends on your opponent playing f3 and g4. Since Black always plays second, it would need three moves for White to achieve a similar mate,

Diagram 35

and would require Black to play f6 followed by g5.

SCHOLAR'S MATE
Diagram 36 is a typical example of Scholar's mate position.

The white Queen has just moved from h5 and captured Black's pawn on f7. Not only is this check, it is also checkmate. The black King cannot capture the invading Queen because he would then be in check from the Bishop on c4, which also attacks the f7 square. There is no room to interpose a piece between White's Queen and Black's King, and the only flight squares available are f8 and e7, both of which are also under fire from the white Queen.

FURTHER EXAMPLES OF CHECKMATE
The next four diagrams give various examples of checkmate. In diagram 37 the white King has been checkmated by the black Rook on e1, his own pawns on f2, g2 and h2 preventing his escape.

In diagram 38 Black's two Bishops effect a mate against the white King with some assistance from their own King.

Diagram 37

Diagram 38

Diagram 36

Diagram 39

Diagram 40

Diagram 41

In diagram 39 the black King has been checkmated by a combination of King, Knight and Bishop, with the white Knight delivering the final check.

In diagram 40 this time it's the lowly pawn on d7 that has delivered the coup de grâce, the black King's escape routes being covered by the white King and the second pawn on e7.

In diagram 41 – the final diagram in this section – I thought it was time for you to do a little thinking of your own. All you have to do is checkmate the black king in one move. The answer is at the beginning of Test your chess IQ (see page 150).

STALEMATE AND OTHER DRAWING MECHANISMS

STALEMATE

This is a position where the person whose turn it is to move cannot do so without placing himself in check, even though he is not actually in check at the time (see diagram 42). As a result, the game is drawn (denoted by the abbreviation = on the score sheet).

If it is Black to move, the game is drawn by

Diagram 42

Diagram 43

stalemate. None of Black's remaining pawns are able to move and the black King cannot move without placing himself in check. If he moves to h6 he will be in check from the Knight on g8 and the pawn on g5. He cannot capture the pawn on h4, for he would then be in check from the pawn on g3, nor can he take the pawn on g5 without being in check by the pawns on h4 and f4.

The position in diagram 42 is taken from a composed problem and is highly unlikely to occur in practice, but that shown in diagram 43 could occur quite easily in an endgame. Having just captured Black's last remaining pawn on f7, White has stalemated his opponent's King. Wherever Black now moves he will put himself in check to the white Queen, yet the King is not actually in check.

Stalemate can be a useful means of avoiding loss in an endgame; so, while you are still at the novice stage I would recommend that you try to play on to the death as much as possible. in that way you will learn a lot first-hand about endgames, and stalemates in particular.

PERPETUAL CHECK

This is another useful means of drawing a game that you would otherwise lose. As the name suggests, it entails being able to check your opponent endlessly, without any possibility of this ever being evaded. Diagram 44 is a simple example of perpetual check. Here White has the worst of it and has decided to bail out. He could now check until eternity if he so chose. The white Queen on h5 checks the King on h8. The black King can only move to g8, so White plays **Qe8+**. Now the King has to move to h7. White returns his Queen to h5+ and so on.

THREEFOLD REPETITION OF THE SAME POSITION

This is a further means of drawing a game and can be claimed if exactly the same position occurs three times. Though not very common it does occur, even at Grandmaster level. The following example, from a game played in 1999 between G Ludden and J Markus, clearly illustrates this mechanism. After both players had completed their 33rd moves the game had reached the position shown in diagram 45.

Diagram 44

Diagram 45

Play continued ...**34.Bc4 Rb8 35.Bb5 Rf8** ... this bringing about the same position as before. (See diagram 46.)

Next came ...**36.Bd3 Rb8 37.Bb5 Rf8** In the final position Black would have claimed the draw before actually making his last move. He would do this by indicating that he was about to repeat the same position for the third time. (See diagram 47.)

AGREEING A DRAW

Another way to effect a draw is simply to agree this with your opponent. In competition chess this occurs usually if neither player believes he or she can win. Accepted procedure is to offer the draw after making your move but before you have stopped your clock. If your opponent accepts, then a simple handshake completes the agreement. However, if the draw is refused, you should write = against your move. Agreed draws are the most common means of securing a drawn game.

THE FIFTY-MOVE RULE

If fifty moves have been made without a pawn being moved or capture made then the game is drawn. although rare at the higher levels of chess this can occur in difficult endings; for example, King, Knight and Bishop versus King and King, and two Knights versus King and pawn.

BASIC TACTICAL KNOWLEDGE

Basic tactical knowledge is what any aspiring army general needs to conduct a campaign of war. What follows are tried and tested methods to divert an enemy force in chess, or to tie him or her down to a particular part of the battlefield.

THE PIN

A simple and very common tactical device, this is used mainly to prevent an opponent's piece or pawn from moving.

Example 1

The position in diagram 48 is arrived at after the following three moves:

1.e4 e6 2.d4 d5 3.Nc3 Bb4 This last move pins the white Knight on c3 to its King – it now cannot move to assist any other part of its army, anywhere on the board, without

Diagram 46

Diagram 47

Diagram 48

Diagram 49

Diagram 50

placing its own King in check. The move puts pressure on White's e4 square and Black therefore threatens to capture the pawn by playing dxe4.

Example 2

In diagram 49 Black has just played **Bb4**, pinning White's Queen to his King. Because the Queen cannot move, as in the previous case, the Queen is now lost. Next move Black can simply capture the Queen on c3, gaining a piece worth nine points for the loss of one worth three.

Bishops seem to do most of the serious pinning, but Rooks and even Queens sometimes get in on the act.

Example 3

In the next position (diagram 50) White has just played his Rook from f1 to e1, pinning Black's Queen to its King. As Black cannot interpose any other piece in this position, once more the mighty Queen is lost to a lesser piece.

Although all the examples given show a piece pinned to a King, you can just as easily pin another piece to a Queen or a Rook, or anything else that may give you some battle advantage. The main thing about a pin is that it hampers the opposition in some way: if the pinned piece moves it will either put its King in check (illegal) or lose material, perhaps even the game.

For more examples of the pin in action see the section Some tactical clues to look for (pages 49–55).

Diagram 51

Diagram 52

Diagram 53

THE FORK

This is a tactical ploy (or, to use chess jargon, motif) in which more than one piece is attacked at the same time. The most common forks are brought about using Knights, but all the other chessmen can be used to fork the enemy.

Example 1

In diagram 51 White has just captured the enemy Queen on d4, only for Black to play **Nc2+**, forking the White Queen, King and Rook (this is called a family fork).

Example 2

In this next example, as shown in diagram 52, it is the black pawn that does the forking, attacking the white Bishop on f4 and the white Knight on d4 at one and the same time.

Example 3

In diagram 53 we have moved on one move from diagram 52.

The Bishop has captured the impudent pawn on e5, but Black plays his Queen to a5, checking White's King on e1 and also attacking the Bishop on e5 (another fork!). In this way Black wins a Bishop for the sacrifice of a pawn.

THE SKEWER

This is rather like a reverse pin. Whereas with a pin the idea is to prevent the front piece from moving, with a skewer the idea is the opposite. Two pieces are attacked on the same line, but in this case the rear of the two is the intended target.

Example 1

Diagram 54 is a simple example of the skewer: the black Rook on e2 attacks the King on e5, forcing it to move, and next move the

Diagram 54

Diagram 55

Rook will be able capture the Queen on e8.

Skewers do not have to involve a King; the two pieces in alignment could be any two pieces.

Example 5

The following position (diagram 55) is taken from one of Nigel Short's games and shows an smart use of two consecutive skewers. Short first played **Be5+**, skewering the black King to the Queen and forcing Black to play **Kxe5** or lose his Queen next move.

Short followed up the first skewer with another, playing **Qc3+**. The black King is again skewered and this time the black Queen – behind it on g7 – is lost. (See diagram 56.)

The last sequence was a demonstration of using two tactical motifs in combination, an essential part of good chess.

Example 6

Diagram 57 shows the start of a lovely sequence by Petrosian, an ex-World Champion, using more than one tactical motif in a great combination that wins the game for him.

Diagram 56

Diagram 57

Diagram 58

Diagram 59

Diagram 60

Diagram 58 shows Petrosian playing **1.Bxe5+**, forking Black's Queen and King.

To avoid the immediate loss of his Queen Black replies **1...Qxe5**. Now Petrosian uses a sacrificial skewer: **2.Qh8+!!** (See diagram 59.)

Black is forced to capture White's Queen or lose his own. And now Petrosian plays a Knight fork **3.Nxf7+**, winning both the Rook on f7 and the Queen on e5. This is an interesting example of a fork followed by a skewer and finished off with another fork. In the game, Black resigned, as the resulting endgame at this expert level is hopelessly lost. (See diagram 60.)

Pins, forks and skewers are the basic building blocks of tactical awareness, but there are others. These extra motifs include back-rank weakness and discovered attacks.

For more examples of the skewer in action see the section Some tactical clues to look for (pages 49–55).

BACK–RANK WEAKNESS

Example

In diagram 61 Black has surrounded his King with foot soldiers, in the shape of pawns,

Diagram 61

Diagram 62

Diagram 63

Diagram 64

Diagram 65

and a full complement of major pieces (both Rooks and his Queen, to do battle with his enemy). Unfortunately this has only served to help him dig his own grave, and White fully exploits this overprotection:

1.Qxb8! White is already threatening to capture the other Rook on f8 with 2.Qxf8+ followed by Re8#. (See diagram 62.)

1...Rxb8 (See diagram 63.)

2.Re8+ (See diagram 64.)

2...Rxe8 3.Rxe8# White has sacrificed his most powerful piece, the Queen (!), to capture the enemy King in his den. (See diagram 65.)

Back-rank mates are very common among beginners and juniors, so be on the lookout. For further examples, see the sections Some tactical clues to look for (pages 49–55) and Test your chess IQ (see pages 150–169).

Diagram 66

Diagram 67

Diagram 68

DISCOVERED ATTACK

This is where one member of your army moves out of the way of another member, allowing both of them to attack two other members of your opponent's army at the same time.

Example

Diagram 66 gives a clear example of a discovered attack. Here, it is worth observing that the black King is on exactly the same file as the white Queen, with only a white Knight preventing a check – a tactical clue to watch out for.

In diagram 67, the white Knight has stepped aside, allowing the Queen to check the enemy King. At the same time, the Knight attacks the black Queen.

To get out of the check, the black King has now moved to e7, and the discovered attack has allowed White's Knight to capture the prize of the enemy Queen. (See diagram 68.)

COMMON MATING PATTERNS

A lot of chess is made up of patterns, that is, proven winning formations to capture the enemy King. Learning these patterns will help to improve your play no end. This section shows a variety of common mating patterns, each of which, or one very similar, will occur at some time in your games.

BACK-RANK MATE

Example 1

Also known as a 'back-ranker', this mate (see diagram 69) occurs when the King is in a position described by the Grandmaster Neil McDonald as 'the coffin'. The white King is trapped behind his pawns on the back rank with no means of escape. It's a very common method of checkmate, especially among novice players.

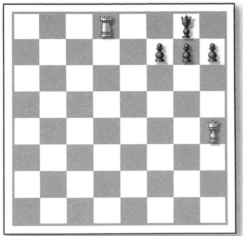

Diagram 69

Diagram 70

Example 2

In diagram 70, Black is to move and cannot escape mate. White threatens simply Qh6 followed by Qg7#. If Black tries Kh7, White plays Qh4+ and then, after Black's response, Qh6, with mate to follow.

DAMIANO'S MATE

The main requirement for this Queen and pawn mate (see diagram 71) is a pawn on g6, although a Bishop would do just as well in this situation.

Example 1

White plays:

1.Rh8+ Kxh8 2.Rh1+ Kg8 3.Rh8+ Kxh8 4.Qh1+ Kg8 5.Qh7#

Example 2

Diagram 72 shows another version of this kind of mating set-up. Here White plays **1.Qh5** threatening an immediate mate by Qh7. Black makes room for his King with **1...Be7** but there follows 2.Qh7+ Kf8 3.Qh8#.

Diagram 71

Diagram 72

Diagram 73

Diagram 74

Diagram 75

MATE WITH QUEEN AND ROOK

The next example is relatively uncomplicatd (see diagram 73). A common method of attack, it involves bludgeoning your way down the open h-file with the two powerhouses of your army; White will ensnare the black King by either Qh7 or Qh8.

MATE WITH QUEEN AND BISHOP

Example 1

The following type of position, as shown in diagram 74, is also very common, but it is important to get the sequence right. I have seen novices try 1.Qxh7+? but the correct method is **1.Bxh7+! Kh8.** The Queen on h5 prevents the black King escaping via f7. White now plays **2.Bg6+,** discovering check by the Queen on h5 and ensuring that the black King cannot escape via f7. There follows **2...Kg8 3.Qh7#.**

Example 2

The following is well worth learning, as there are two different mating patterns here: mate in three moves and mate in two:
1.Bg6+ Kg8 2.Qh7+ Kf8 3.Qf7#
Or
1.Bf5+ Kg8 2.Be6# (See diagram 75.)

MATING PATTERNS INVOLVING A ROOK AND A KNIGHT

Example 1

In diagram 76 White can play 1.Nf6+ Kf8 2.Rf7# or 1.Nf6+ Kh8 2.Rh7#.

Example 2

In diagram 77 White plays **1.Rd8# Kf7 2.Rf8#.** (The Knight not only protects the Rook but also stops Black's King escaping to e7.) Or White can play 1.Rd8+ Kh7 2.Rh8#.

MATING PATTERNS INVOLVING A QUEEN AND KNIGHT

Example 1: Smothered mate
The following sequence leads to a smothered mate which is known as Philidor's Legacy. In your own games you may not be able to secure this specific mate but even the threat of it may well help you to gain a material advantage over your opponent. I have seen this exact mate carried out in a junior county match and won with it once myself when I was still at school. (See diagram 78.)

1.Nf7+ Kg8 2.Nh6++ Double check.

2...Kh8 (If Black plays **2...Kf8** White replies **3.Qf7#**.)

3.Qg8+!! R (or N)xg8 4.Nf7#

Example 2
The next is a fairly typical Queen and Knight mating attack against the castled King. If Black moves his Rook to, say, d8, White just plays **Qh7+** followed by **Qh8#** or **Qxf7#**. See diagram 79.)

Diagram 77

Diagram 78

Diagram 76

Diagram 79

Diagram 80

Diagram 81

Diagram 82

Example 3

Diagram 80 shows a similar mating attack to the last, but here Black has pawns on g7 and f7 instead of f7 and e7. If Black plays **1...Rfd8** White now replies: **2.Qxf7+ Kh8 3.Ne6 Rg8 4.Qh5#.**

MATING PATTERNS INVOLVING A QUEEN, KNIGHT AND BISHOP

Example: Greco's mate

Another mating attack, known as Greco's mate, is based on similar principles to those explored above. In this position Black can only avoid immediate disaster by **1...h6.** White continues with **2.Bxf7+ Kh8 3.Qg6,** threatening mate with Qh7. There follows **3...hxg5 4.Qh5#.** (See diagram 81.)

MATING PATTERNS INVOLVING A BISHOP AND ROOK

Example 1

In diagram 82 Black somehow has to parry White's threat of Rg5#. His only hope of escape is to move his Rook, let's say to a8. White checks anyway.

1.Rg5+ Kf8 2.Rg7!. The point is that Black cannot avoid White now playing 3.Rxh7 and 4.Rh8#, his pieces and pawns all being in each other's way. Having space to move is vitally important; imagine firing an arrow among a crowd of your fellow soldiers!

Example 2

The following position shows another successful assault on an entrenched King position. Black may seem safe here but White, simply by sacrificing his Queen, can rip open his opponent's defences and the enemy King is soon captured:

1.Qxf6! gf6 2.Rg3+ Kh8 3.Bxf6#. (See diagram 83.)

Example 3

Next we have two evenly matched armies – a King, a Rook and a lone Bishop facing a King, three pawns and a Rook – but White strikes first. (See diagram 84.)

1.Rxg7+ Kh8 2.Rxf7+! It would be a mistake now to play 2.Rg5+, for Black would get in a counterblow 2...f6! Always ensure that you destroy any possible resistance. In this case, by removing one of Black's key defenders, Rxf7+ White does just that.

2...Kg8 3.Rg7+ Kh8 And now:

4.Rg5+! The black King is entombed in the corner and can only delay the final blow by sacrificing his Rook.

4...Rf6 5.Bxf6#

MATING PATTERNS INVOLVING TWO ROOKS ON THE SEVENTH RANK

Following on from the last diagram we have two white Rooks powerfully positioned on the seventh rank. One Rook on the seventh rank, deep in enemy territory, nearly always causes trouble but two together can wreak havoc. White, to move, can achieve mate very quickly:

1.Rg7+ Kh8 2.Rh7+ Kg8 Rcg7# (See diagram 85.)

Diagram 83

Diagram 84

Diagram 85

Diagram 86

THE EPAULETTE MATE

Diagram 86 illustrates one of the less common mating patterns: the epaulette mate. The Rooks here look like the epaulettes on a general's jacket.

MATING PATTERNS INVOLVING PAWNS

Next it is the turn of the lowly foot soldier to deliver the *coup de grâce*. (See diagram 87.)

1.g6 This pawn helps threaten Qh7#, as the pawn supports its Queen in the final assault.

1...Bg8 To defend the weak h7 square.

2.g7#

MATING PATTERNS INVOLVING KNIGHT AND BISHOP

Diagram 88 shows how just a Knight and Bishop, assisted by some unfortunately placed defenders, can effect mate on their own.

1.Nxf7+ Kg8 2.Nh6#
Or
1.Ng6+ Kg8 2.Ne7#

Diagram 87

Diagram 88

Diagram 89

Diagram 90   **Diagram 91**

In diagram 89 White plays 1.Be6, with the threat of Bd4#, and after 1...d4 2.Bh2, the lethal threat of the second Bishop checkmating on the other diagonal can only be delayed.

EXAMPLES FROM TOURNAMENT PLAY

The next three positions are taken from tournament matches and all have some practical merit in them. You are unlikely ever to find yourself in identical positions but similar structures will certainly occur, so be aware.

Example 1

The game shown in diagram 90 was played in 1869 between McDonell and Boden. Boden now unleashed **Qc3+!!** And after White recaptured, Boden replied **Ba3#**. This mating attack is always a good possibility when your opponent castles on the Queenside (0–0–0) and plays c3 (or c6 if he is Black).

Example 2

Legal, teacher of the celebrated chess master Philidor, gave us this little gem as long ago as 1750. The game, short though it is, is instructive. (See diagram 91.)

1.e4 e5 2.Nf3 d6 3.Bc4 Bg4 It's safer to develop Knights before Bishops!

4.Nc3 g6? Neglecting to get his army out of bed.

5.Nxe5! Bxd1? Pure greed.

6.Bxf7+ Ke7 7.Nd5#

Remember that the object of the exercise in chess is to mate the enemy King. Treasure-hunting while your army remains undeveloped could result in the loss of your King's crown.

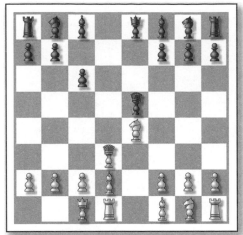

Diagram 92

Example 3
The final example comes from a game between Reti and Tartakover played in Vienna in 1911. I never cease to be amazed by the fact that even the strongest Grandmasters can sometimes forget the advice they were given when they first learned chess. Here Tartakover still has his King stuck in the centre; his Queen is already out in the centre of the board, even though only eight moves have been played; and, worst of all, he has neglected his development. Reti punished him severely. (See diagram 92.)

9.Qd8+!! Kxd8 10.Bg5++ Kc7 11.Bd8#

Had Tartakover tried 10...Ke8, Reti would have finished him off with 11.Rd8#. Try to remember this final position when you come to the Test your chess IQ section later in this book (see pages 150–169).

A MATING PATTERN FROM A NOVEL

The following position comes from the novel, Anastasia and Chess. (See diagram 93.)

Diagram 93

1.Ne7+ Kh8 2.Rxh7+ Kxh7 3.Rh5#

Diagram 94

Diagram 95

Diagram 96

Diagram 97

'CORRIDOR MATE'

A checkmate similar to that considered above is one that I like to think of as a 'corridor mate'. (See diagram 94.)

1.Qg5 Kh8 2.Qh6 Rg8 3.Qxh7+ Kxh7 4.Rh3#

And, finally, another 'corridor mate'.

1.Ng6+ hxg6 2.Rh4# (**See** diagram 95.)

SOME TACTICAL CLUES TO LOOK FOR

In chess you need to act like a general and think like a detective. Tactical clues appear frequently during games but you need to be able to spot them, so you must be constantly on the lookout for the sort of ploys we've discussed: forks (see page 36), pins (see pages 34–35), skewers (see pages 36–37) and such like. Clues to these include King and Queen on the same diagonal or line; pieces separated by a potential Knight fork, undefended pieces and many others. You won't be able to spot all of these straight away but with practice and experience you will notice them increasingly quickly.

UNGUARDED PIECES

In diagram 96 White has spotted that his opponent's King cannot move to g8 (because this square is covered by White's Bishop standing on b3) and that the squares g7 and g6 are blocked. A check on the file should therefore win the game, but how should he manage this without giving Black an opportunity to defend such a threat? The tactical clue here is the unguarded black Queen on c7. So, **1.Bxb6!** This move attacks the Queen while at the same time – and the same time is the important bit – threatens to play the white Queen to h3#. Black cannot defend both threats at once and must lose his Queen for a Bishop if he is to avoid checkmate.

In diagram 97 the tactical clue is the same as before: the unguarded black Queen (this time on a5). How can you exploit this? The black King has no square to move to; a check should finish him off. So **1.Nd5!** The white Queen on d2 now attacks the unguarded Queen on a5. At the same time, and more importantly, White threatens mate by 2.Ne7. It is impossible for Black to prevent the simultaneous threats; to prevent checkmate he must again lose his Queen.

Diagram 98

Diagram 99

Diagram 100

THE PIN

Example 1: A pin and fork

Your clue in diagram 98 is the pin on the Bishop standing on e6. Now **1.d5!** forks the black Bishop and Knight on c6. Because of the pin Black cannot safely capture the errant pawn with his Queen (1...Qxd5? 2.Qxd5).

Example 2: A pin and back-rank weakness

In diagram 98, a position taken from a game between Evans (White) and Bisguier in the US Championship of 1957, the clues are the weakness of Black's back rank and the fact that the black King is hemmed in by his own pawns while the Queen on e7 is pinned by White's Queen on a3. Exploiting the pin on the black Queen, White now played **1.Bc6!!** If Black captures the white Queen, **1...Qxa3**, Black simply replies **2.Rxe8#**. And if instead Black replies **1...Bxc6**, then **2.Qxe7+ Kg8 3.Qe8+ Bxe8 4.Rxe8#**. (See diagram 99.)

Example 3: A pin involving major pieces on the same diagonal

In diagram 100 the clue is Black's King and Queen both being on the same diagonal – ripe for a pin. **1.Bc5** (pin number 1) or 1.Bb6! (pin number 2). Black counters the first pin with one of his own. White then plays **2.Qf4+!** – exploiting his pin on the Black Queen and, because of his now double attack on the enemy Queen, White will next be able to play **3.Qxd6**, winning the black Queen for free.

Example 4: A pin involving a pawn promotion

In diagram 101 White could promote his pawn standing on d7 if it were not for the black Rook attacking it from d5. The clue to victory is the fact of the black Rook and King in line on the fifth rank – all you need to force your pawn home is a pin on the black Rook, to prevent it from moving: **1.Rg5!** Now if 1...Rxg5 2.d8 =Q+, also forking the black Rook and King.

Example 5: A pin involving an unguarded piece and a sacrifice

In the next position White is a sacrificed piece down, but has a forced win available. There are several clues to notice here: The black King is still in the centre while White's is safely castled; the Knight on c6 is pinned by the white Queen to the black King; the black Queen is only defended by a Knight on f6. How can you exploit these factors? The key clue is that Black Queen has only the Knight to defend it. If White could find a way of taking that Knight with check then the black Queen would fall. So...

1.Rd8+! This sacrifice of the Rook forces the enemy King on to d8 and the same diagonal as both his Knight on f6 and White's Bishop on g5. The rest is easy:

1...Kxd8 2.Bxf6+ The necessary check. And next:

3.Qxe5. (See diagram 102.) Of course, you could also use the fact that after 1...Kxd8 the Knight on f6 is pinned and just 2.Qxe5 wins the game.

KNIGHT FORK

Example 1: A Knight fork and skewer

Diagram 103 needs more detective work.

On the surface Black appears to be winning: he is better developed, his King is in safety, and he threatens to play Qxh1, winning White's Rook. The clue here is the fact that the square d5, and g8 on which the

Diagram 101

Diagram 102

Diagram 103

black King now stands, are separated by a Knight fork on the e7 square. So, all we have to do is force the black Queen to d5:

1.Qd5! This skewers the Queen and the Rook standing on a8. If 1...Qxd5, then 2.Nxe7+ wins the Queen. And if 1...Q moves then Black plays 2.Qxa8. Either way White finishes ahead on material.

The key word in the above puzzle is force. Your opponent won't dance to your tune just because you wish him to; you have to make him do so.

Example 2: A fork involving destroying the guard

In diagram 104 it is Black's turn to spot the clues. What he'd like to do is fork White's King and Queen by playing Ne2+, but the Bishop on f3 guards that square. If that's all the problem is then all we have to do is destroy the guard: **1.Rxf3!** Now if 1...Rxf3, then 2.Ne2+ wins White's Queen.

Example 3: Engineering a fork

Next, another fork clue: In diagram 105 White's Rook and Bishop are separated by a Knight fork. All we need to calculate is how to get the black Knight to e4 without losing

any time: **1...Ng5+ 2.Kd7 (or e7) Rxd6! And after 3.Kxd6 Ne4+** wins White's Rook and it's child's play from there to push home the two connected passed pawns.

OVERLOADING

Example 1: An overloaded Rook

In diagram 106 Black's Rook is overloaded; it is trying to protect the back rank while also guarding his Queen on d5. **1.Re8+** is the 'straw that breaks the camel's back'. **1...Rxe8** is forced (there's that important word again), and **2.Qxd5** leaves White with a large material advantage.

Example 2: An overloaded Queen

In diagram 107 it's the white Queen that is overloaded. The poor thing is trying to protect her Knight on e2 and the square f4 from invasion by Black's Rook. We need the destruction squad in again: **1...Qxe2+ 2.Qxe2 Rf4#.**

The lesson here is a simple one: if your opponent is guarding an important square with a piece, often the only way for your army to advance and invade is to destroy the defender.

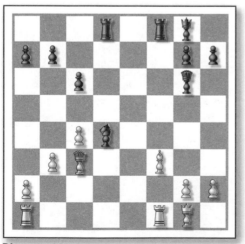

Diagram 104

Diagram 105

Diagram 106

Diagram 107

Example 3

If you have managed to understand the last lesson then you should find this next example easy to understand. The clue here, a big one, is the alignment of White's Queen and Bishop along the diagonal a1–h8, aiming right at g7 and a threatened checkmate. But Black has a Knight posted on e6 guarding that square. The answer? Exterminate the Knight!**1.Rxe6 Qxe6 2.Qxg7#**. (See diagram 108.)

DEFLECTION

As you won't always be able to destroy the guarding piece you will need other means of breaking through at your disposal. In diagram 109 the white Knight on e3 is guarding the square f1, preventing Black from capturing (checkmating) the enemy King. What you need here is a deflection or decoy: **1.Rxd1+!** deflects the guard – the Knight on e3 – from minding the f1 square. There follows **1...Nxd1 2.Qf1#**. (See diagram 109.)

Diagram 108

Diagram 109

Diagram 110

Diagram 111

Diagram 112

INTERFERENCE

Example 1

This example involves not only some more deflection work but also some interference. Black obviously thinks he's got his King safely tucked up on g8, but in fact the King is too tightly tucked up. If we could somehow remove Black's defence of the notoriously weak square, f7, then the battle would be won. So, **1.Re7!** This move threatens an immediate Qf7# and also opens the diagonal a2–g8 for White's Queen to give check on d5. If Black's Bishop or Knight take the Rook on e7 they will interfere with the black Queen's protection of f7. If 1.Qxe7 then …Qd5+ 2.Qf7 Qxf7#. This time the Queen has been deflected from guarding d5. In a way White has also exploited the black Queen's overload as well! (See diagram 110.)

Example 2

The position in diagram 111 could be tricky unless you recognize the all-important clue: King and Queen on the same file. When this occurs there is always a good chance of a pin or a skewer. In this case there is a potential pin by **1.Re2!** But what if **1…Qxe2?** Well, and this is probably the hard bit to spot, the black Queen is then deflected from guarding d5. There follows **2.Qd5+ Ke8** (forced!) then **3.Qe6+ Kd8** (forced!) and **4.Qe7#**.

STALEMATE

Example 1

Sometimes when you have taken a bit of a beating it's time to look for a draw, a stalemate possibility. Imagine yourself in the position shown in diagram 112. You are a Rook and Bishop behind and your King has nowhere to move. And that is just the clue you need! Not only has your King no squares available but the pawns cannot move either.

All you have to do, therefore, is force White to capture your Queen. So, **1...Qa2+!
2.Kxa2** – stalemate, and you've saved your bacon.

Example 2

This next example, as shown in diagram 113, is more difficult but the clue is the same: the White King is trapped (fortunately!) on b4. Without this potential stalemate Black would soon win by promoting his pawn (1...g1=Q). However White still has to get rid of his Queen and his Rook. The answer? **1.Rc8+ Rxc8** (forced!) **2.Qa7+ Kxa7** (forced!) – stalemate.

Diagram 113

BACK-RANK WEAKNESS

Example 1

The clue here is simply the weak back rank itself. In diagram 114 Black's back rank is astonishingly vulnerable (having no major pieces to defend it at all) – a position brought about by the skill of Alekhine, World Champion from 1927–35 and 1937–46. Alekhine continued:

1.Rxf8+! Kxf8 (forced) **2.Qd8#**

Diagram 114

Example 2

In the final position in this section, a game played in 1994, White again has very little protection for his back rank; his Rook on e2 helps to incarcerate the King and the only defence against an invasion by Black's Rook is the Knight on g3, so **1...Qxg3!**. Neither 2.Qxg3 nor fxg3 prevents the mate on h1. (See diagram 115.)

Diagram 115

OPENINGS

A chess game begins with the opening. There are simple principles to be understood and it is necessary to be familiar with the openings for both Black and White. You also need to know what traps to watch out for and what to do if you're faced with an opening you've never seen.

OCCUPYING THE CENTRE

In real-life battles each side in the conflict will usually seek out the high ground. From here it is possible to look down on one's enemy and have an all-round view of what's going on. In chess, of course, there is no high ground; its equivalent is the centre of the board – specifically the squares e4, d4, e5 and d5.

It is these four squares that strong players fight most fiercely for, though adjacent squares (c4, c5, f4 and f5) are also of some importance. Players often strive to occupy the centre squares with pawns. If you can do this without being easily driven off, and of course have no other obvious weaknesses, you will certainly gain some advantage. Diagram 116 shows a typical position four moves into the Giucco Piano (see page 60), there is already a battle going on for control of the centre squares. White has developed a Knight to f3 to attack the d4 and e5; the pawn on c3 attacks d4; another pawn occupies e4, from where it also applies pressure to d5; and the white Bishop on c4, as well as targeting the weak square f7, also puts pressure on d5. Black, for his part, has developed two Knights, the one on f6 attacking the squares e4 and d5, and the one on c6 attacking d4 while defending e5; the Bishop on c5 attacks White's weak f2 square and also applies

pressure to d4, with assistance from his pawn on e5.

THE HYPERMODERN APPROACH TO THE CENTRE

Having occupation of the centre is a classical chess theme, but some players prefer the so-called hypermodern openings, in which the opposition is allowed to occupy the centre, with a view to attacking and destroying this later. The aim in such openings is to control the centre from afar.

The following is a position from the Modern Defence. Here Black – in true hypermodern style – has let White take up residence in the centre, intending to undermine this as the game progresses. (See diagram 117.)

THE IMPORTANCE OF RAPID DEVELOPMENT

As with all battles your army is not much use if it is slow to get out of bed. You cannot fight a successful campaign with most of your men still fast asleep in the barracks. Put another way, get your men off the back line and into battle formation as quickly as possible. Chess players refer to this as rapid development. Even Grandmasters occasionally forget this simple principle and often pay the price.

It is generally considered better to

develop your Knights before Bishops. This is because Bishops are long-range pieces and it is often unclear where best to place them until a few moves of the game have been played.

Diagram 118 shows a typical position after five moves in a variation of the Sicilian Defence. Both players have already developed their Knights; only now will they elect where to place their Bishops.

The Queen is such a powerful piece that she is best left at home in the early stages of the game, lest she be surrounded and lost! Like the Queen, Rooks (Castles) are considered to be major pieces, but they start the game tucked away in the corners. It is therefore a good idea to castle early so that they can take part in the coming battle where necessary.

ADVICE

AIM to occupy or control the centre.

DEVELOP your pieces as rapidly as possible.

VERY early development of your Queen is dangerous.

IT'S usually a mistake to move a piece twice before moving all your other pieces once! (Note the pawns are not classified as pieces.)

CASTLE as early as possible to get your King into safety and your Rooks into battle.

EACH side has a weak square – f2 for White and f7 for Black.

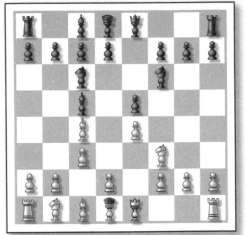

Diagram 116

Diagram 117

Diagram 118

OPENINGS FOR WHITE

When chess players refer to openings they are not thinking of the twenty different first moves with which it is possible to begin a game. An opening to an experienced player is a whole series of moves, which have evolved over a long period of time. Some of these, like the Ruy Lopez (see page 71) and Giucco Piano (see below), have taken several hundred years to reach the level they are at now, and they are still evolving. Chess continues to develop and new ideas in the opening are appearing all the time. It is impossible in the confines of this book to acquaint you thoroughly with even the small selection of openings that follow; for that you would need at least one specialized book on each. However, I believe the lines given here will enable you to play certain openings with confidence. To help you understand how each may develop I have included at least one full game for every line, but my notes generally finish at the end of the opening phase. but it will at least give you an idea.

The two most common first moves are 1.e4 and 1.d4, so I propose to concentrate on these. Each can lead to myriad of different openings.

KING-PAWN OPENINGS
(Open games)

Let's begin with the opening that most beginners learn first.

Giucco Piano

1.e4 e5 White's first move stakes a claim for the central square (e4), attacks a square in Black's half of the board (d5) and releases the Queen and King Bishop to take part in any early skirmishes. Black responds similarly, staking a claim to the important central square (e5) and targeting d4 in White's half of the board.

2.Nf3 Nc6 White attacks the black pawn on e5 and at the same time counters Black's pressure on d4. Black defends his pawn and increases the pressure on d4.

3.Bc4 Bc5 White targets the weak square, f7, and further pressurizes d5. Again Black responds in kind and targets White's f2.

At this point there are several ways for White to react: he can play the simple developing move, 4.Nc3; he can support the pawn on e4 by playing 4.d3, which also releases the other Bishop; he can play 4.b4, the Evans Gambit (which we'll look at next) or he can play 4.c3, preparing to play 5.d4 and staking full claim to the centre before Black can get all his pieces mobilized. This move offers a real challenge to Black. He will have to think carefully before his next move.

4.c3 Nf6 Most moves have a down as well as an up side. The down side for White's 4.c3 is that, temporarily, it deprives his Queenside Knight of its natural square, c3. Black's logical response, therefore, is to accept White's challenge and attack the undefended pawn standing on e4.

5.d3 A sound move, this is probably White's best reply. It supports the e4 pawn and prepares for the advance d4 later in the game when White is safely castled. The main alternatives are 5.d4!? and 5.b4. With 5.d4 White intends a sharp tactical battle – one that often gets good results up to club level, but that is no longer considered best against a player well versed in the theory of this line. 5.b4 aims to gain space (territory) and push Black back on the Queenside.

The following game, played between two strong players, is based on some original analysis by Greco – one the great early players of the game – and illustrates how this opening may develop.

BLAUERT, J (2290)–SCHMITTDIEL, E (2425)

FRG-ch qual Koenigslutter1988

1.e4 e5 2.Nf3 Nc6 3.d4 exd4 4.Bc4 Bc5 5.c3 Nf6 (See diagram 119.)

6.cxd4 Bb4+ 7.Nc3 Nxe4 White decides to jettison a pawn in favour of rapid development and control of the centre. (See diagram 120.)

8.0–0 Bxc3 9.d5! This essential move is the beginning of a variation known as the Moller attack. (See diagram 121.)

9...Ne5 10.bxc3 Nxc4 11.Qd4 Forking the two Black Knights.

11...Ncd6 12.Qxg7 Qf6 Indirectly defending the Rook on h8.

13.Qxf6 Nxf6 14.Re1+ Kf8 15.Bh6+ Kg8 Black's King is now trapped and all White needs is an appropriate check to finish his opponent off.

16.Re5 Threatening mate on g5.

16...Nde4 Defending the threatened mate.

17.Nd2 Black resigns because he cannot avoid being mated. If 17...Nxd2, White replies 18.Rg5#, and if 17...d6, there follows 18.Nxe4 dxe5 19.Nf6#.

1–0

Diagram 119

Diagram 120

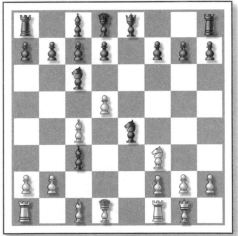

Diagram 121

The Evans Gambit

The Evans Gambit was first introduced to the chess world in about 1826 by its originator, Captain W D Evans. It's an aggressive variation of the Giucco Piano.

Example

The following game is typical of the caveman-style approach needed to play the Evans Gambit properly.

DE RIVIERIE, J–JOURNOUD
Paris 1860

1.e4 e5 2.Nf3 Nc6 3.Bc4 Bc5 4.b4!? This is the move that typifies the Evans Gambit. The idea of the move b4 is to distract Black's attention from the centre. (See diagram 122.)

4...Bxb4 5.c3 Having distracted Black, White now sets about gaining full control.

5...Ba5 6. d4 exd4 7.0–0 Developing pieces is nearly always the number one priority, especially in a gambit opening.

7...Nf6 8.Ba3! This is a vital move, as it keeps the enemy King stuck in the centre.

8...d6 An attempt by Black to get into safety.

9.e5! By attacking Black's Knight on f6 and the loyal pawn on d6 at the same time, White maintains the pressure on the Black army.

9...dxe5 10.Qb3 And now the Queen and Bishop line up along the diagonal a2–g8, aiming at the weak f7 square.

10...Qd7 11.Re1 Another member of White's artillery joins in the attack; Black is given no let-up. Almost all of White's pieces are coordinated in their assault on the black King, whereas Black's Bishop, out on a5, can hardly give any assistance in defence, while the white-squared Bishop and the Rook on a8 haven't yet got out of bed.

11...e4 12.Nbd2 Bxc3 13.Nxe4 Bxe1 14.Rxe1 Kd8 Desperately trying to get out of the line of fire.

15.Neg5 Na5 16.Ne5 Nxb3 17.Nexf7+ Qxf7 18.Nxf7+Kd7 19.Bb5+c6 20.Re7# (See diagram 123.)

1–0

Diagram 122

Diagram 123

It is well worth examining the final position: some members of Black's army – both the Rooks and the white-squared Bishop – have yet to move from their posts.

The Two Knights' Defence

This is another opening that beginners are often taught early in their chess careers. A sound opening system, it is still used at Grandmaster level. One way of dealing with it from White's point of view, which is illustrated in the game below, is known as The Fried Liver Attack (its real name is The Fegatello)!

LOTTER, B–HERTEL, H
Bayern-chB (Women) Tirschenreuth, 1982

1.e4 e5 2.Nf3 Nc6 3.Bc4 Nf6 4.Ng5
White begins by targeting the weak f7 square. This variation is about all-out attack, before Black can settle his forces. (See diagram 124.)

Diagram 124

4...d5 5.exd5 Nxd5 6.Nxf7 White forks the black Queen and the Rook on h8; Black is forced to capture, or else lose material. This forces the black King out into the open. (See diagram 125.)

Diagram 125

6...Kxf7 7.Qf3+ By checking with the Queen from f3 White attacks the black King and the Knight on d5. Again Black has little option but to move his King to e6, adding some extra protection to the beleaguered Knight. (See diagram 126.)

7...Ke6 8.Nc3 This poor Knight is now attacked three times: by White's Knight on c3, by the Queen and by the Bishop.

8...Ncb4 This defends the black Knight three times, balancing out attack and defence, and also threatening 9...Nc2+.

Diagram 126

Diagram 127

Diagram 128

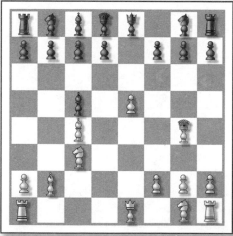

Diagram 129

9.Qe4 c6 10.a3 Driving away one of Black's defenders of the pinned Knight on d5.

10...Na6 11.d4 Bd6 12.f4 Nac7 13.fxe5 Be7 14.0–0 Rf8 15.Qg4+Rf5 16.Qxf5# The battle is over; Black's King is caught almost in mid-board. (See diagram 127.)

1–0

The Danish Gambit

This opening belongs to the Romantic period of chess, when attack and sacrifices were all. This opening is no longer played at the highest level, not because it is unsound but because with best play it leads to an early draw. It is well worth experimenting with, however, up to club level.

KOPCZYNSKI, M–CLAPA, T
Polish Championships – U12
Kolobrzeg, 2001

1.e4 e5 2.d4 exd4 3.c3 dxc3 4.Bc4 cxb2

5.Bxb2 White concedes two pawns for open lines of attack for his two Bishops and easy development of the remainder of his army. (See diagram 128.)

5...Nf6 6.Nc3 Bc5 7.e5 This pawn advance drives back Black's Knight and gains space (control of Black's d6 and f6 squares) in Black's half of the board.

7...Ng8 8.Qg4 White's 11th move, by attacking the pawn on g7, creates a little weakness in his enemy's position: after

11...g6 the black squares f6 and h6 are 'holes', entry points for White's army. (See diagram 129.)

8...g6 9.Qf4 Targeting the weak f7 square.
9...f5 10.Ne4 If 10...fxe4, then 11.Qf7#.

10...Qe7 11.e6 This advance brings White's black-square Bishop on b2 to life; 12.Bxh8 is threatened. (See diagram 130.)

11...fxe4 12.Qf7+ Kd8 13.Bxh8 Nh6 14.Qxe7+Kxe7 15.exd7 Bxd7 16.Ne2 e3 17.f3 Nc6 18.Bc3 Bb4 19.Rb1 Bxc3+ 20.Nxc3 b6 21.Nd5+Kd6 22.Nxe3 Nf5 23.Rd1+ Kc5 24.Rxd7 Nxe3 25.Bf1 Nd5 26.a3 Nd4 27.Bd3 Nf4 28.Be4 Nxg2+ 29.Kf2 Nf4 30.Bxa8 Nd3+31.Ke3 Ne5 32.Rxc7+ Kd6 33.Kxd4

1–0

The Scotch Game

This is one of those openings that once seemed to have been consigned to the past, until the then world number one, Garry Kasparov, gave it the kiss of life. The Scotch Game now figures in the repertoire of many a Grandmaster.

MOROZEVICH, A (2630)–HUZMAN, A (2580)
Donner Memorial, Amsterdam, 1995

1.e4 e5 2.Nf3 Nc6 3.d4 exd4 4.Nxd4
The commencement of the Scotch Game. White's prime idea here is to make an early assault on Black's e-pawn before he has time to strengthen the square e5 with moves like d6 and so on. (See diagram 131.)

4...Nf6 Black gets on with his development and attacks the white pawn on e4.

5.Nxc6 bxc6 6.e5 With these few moves White attempts to drive off Black's centralized Knight.

6...Qe7 By pinning the pawn temporarily Black hopes to make White's position as uncomfortable as possible.

7.Qe2 Nd5 8.c4 Ba6 Now Black pins the c4 pawn to White's Queen. It is always a good idea to play moves that keep your opponent under fire.

9.g3 0–0–0 So, for a change, it is White who lags behind in development. Black's King is in relative safety and he has developed four pieces. White has only two pieces developed and his King is still in the centre.

Diagram 130

Diagram 131

10.b3 f6 11.Bg2 fxe5 White gladly sacrifices this pawn to catch up on development.

12.0–0 Nf6 13.Ba3 By developing with tempo (see Glossary, page 190), attacking the enemy Queen, he gains a little time for his future plans.

13...Qe6 14.Qd2 e4 15.Qa5 c5 16.Bxc5 Bxc5 17.Qxc5 Qb6 18.Qxb6 axb6 White has regained his gambit pawn and material is level once more. Furthermore, the pawn on e4 is weak, as it cannot easily be defended by a friendly pawn. This is the end of the opening phase of the game.

The game continues:
19.Re1 Rhe8 20.Nc3 Bb7 21.a4 d5 22.cxd5 Bxd5 23.a5 bxa5 24.Rxa5 Bb7 25.Rb5 Rd6 26.Na4 Bc6 27.Ra5 Kd8 28.Rc1 Re7 29.b4 Bd5 30.Nc3 Bb7 31.h4 Rb6 32.b5 Re5 33.Re1 Rc5 34.Ra3 Rc4 35.Bf1 Rd4 36.Na4 Rbd6 37.Nc5 Bd5 38.Rc1 Rd2 39.Ra7 e3 40.fxe3 Nh5 41.e4 Rg6 42.exd5 Rxg3+ 43.Kh1 Rg4 44.Ra3 Rxh4+ 45.Bh3 Rxd5 46.Re3 (See diagram 132.)

White threatens 47.Nb7#. If 46...c6, there follows 47.Nb7+ Kc7 48.Rc6+ Kxb7 49.Re7+ Kb8 50.Rc8#.

1–0

The Scotch Gambit

This is a more adventurous form of the Scotch Game, and more suited to those with a swashbuckling nature.

SHUMOV, I–VON JAENISCH, C
Russia, 1850

1.e4 e5 2.Nf3 Nc6 3.d4 exd4 4.Bc4 White refrains from recapturing on d4 and ·gets on with bringing his army rapidly into play. (See diagram 133.)

4...Bc5 Think back to Some tactical clues to loof for (see pages 49–55). The Bishop is unguarded on this square.

5.Ng5 Nh6 6.Nxf7 Diagram 134 shows the Knight forking the black Queen and Rook on h8, forcing Black's reply. It is better to play moves that compel your opponent to make a certain move, rather than just hoping they will.

Diagram 132

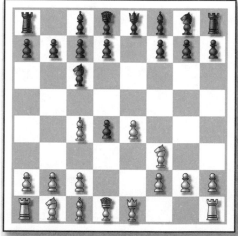

Diagram 133

6...Nxf77.Bxf7+Kxf7 8.Qh5+ From here the white Queen attacks the unguarded Bishop on c5. (See diagram 135.)

8...g6 9.Qxc5 d6 10.Qb5 Re8 11.0–0 In keeping with the true nature of gambit play White ignores his attacked pawn on e4 and prepares to bring more troops into the action.

11...Rxe4 12.Qd5+Re6 13.Bg5Qe8 14.f4 Kg7 15.f5 (See diagram 136.)

15...Re5 16.f6+ Kh8 17.f7 Kg7 18.fxe8(N)+ (See diagram 137.)

A key moment; White can win in many different ways, but this is the neatest, and demonstrates clearly when to promote to something other than a Queen. By taking a Knight, White calls check. This then forces Black to deal with the situation immediately, or he has lost the game.

18...Rxe8 19.Qf7+Kh8 20.Bf6#

1–0

A mating pattern worth remembering.

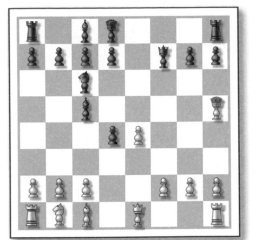

Diagram 135

Diagram 136

Diagram 134

Diagram 137

Diagram 138

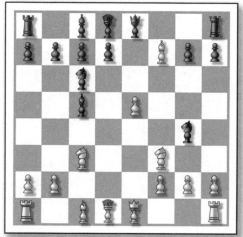

Diagram 139

Diagram 140

The Goring Gambit

This is another of those openings no longer played at the very highest level. However, the Grandmaster Jonathan Penrose, winner of the British Championship a record nine times, used it to defeat many an unwary opponent.

EVERETT, M–LABINER, J
Detroit, 1991

1.e4 e5 2.Nf3 Nc6 3.d4 exd4 4.c3 dxc3 5.Nxc3 The defining moment in the Goring Gambit: White has sacrificed a pawn for the free use of the half-open d- and c-files and rapid development. (See diagram 138.)

5...Bc5 6.Bc4 Nf6 7.e5 Ng4 8.Bxf7+ It's that weak f7 square again. If Black plays 8...Kxf7, White replies 9.Ng5+, followed by 10.Qxg5, regaining the gambit pawn with a withering attack. (See diagram 139.)

8...Kf8 9.0–0 White continues calmly to develop the remainder of his army.

9...Ncxe5 10.Nxe5 Nxe5 11.Bb3 d6 12.Ne4 Bf5 13.Bg5 Qe8 14.Nxc5 dxc5 15.Qd5 White threatens 16.Qxc5+ Qe7 17.Qxe7#. Black's King is still stuck in the centre and his Rook on h8 cannot take part in the battle. (See diagram 140.)

15...b6 16.Rfe1 Black resigns; he cannot save his lonely Knight on e5 and the battle is effectively over.

1–0

The King's Gambit (declined)

This is another opening popular in the Romantic period (see the 'Evergreen Game' in The middlegame, pages 116–117), but unlike many others it is still popular with some modern-day Grandmasters.

RETI, R–BARASZ, Z
Temesvar, 1912

1.e4 e5 2.f4 The start of the King's Gambit: White attempts to persuade Black to capture his f-pawn, to give himself not only free rein in the centre (ideally White would like to occupy both e4 and d4 with pawns), but also a useful half-open file to bring further pressure to bear on Black's f7 square.

2...Bc5 Black declines the gambit. (See diagram 141.)

3.Nf3 d6 4.c3 Bg4 By pinning the white Knight Black puts indirect pressure on White's d4 square: if White now attempts to play 5.d4 Black can reply 5...Bxf3 and White will be obliged to reply gxf3, shattering his Kingside pawn structure, or else lose a pawn. (See diagram 142.)

5.fxe5 dxe5 6.Qa4+ White removes himself from the awkward pin by giving check.

6...Bd7 This is forced; otherwise White can play 7.Nxe5.

7.Qc2 Qe7 8.d4 Bd6 9.Bg5 Nf6 10.Nbd2 Nc6 11.Bc4 0-0-0 12.0-0 h6 13.Bxf6 gxf6 (See diagram 143.)

The game now passes out of the opening into the middlegame and the remainder of the game is given without notes. However, White has succeeded in one of his primary aims and opened up the f-file to his advantage.

Diagram 141

Diagram 142

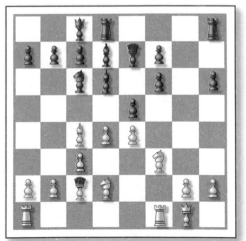

Diagram 143

14.d5 Nb8 15.b4 Rdg8 16.Nh4 Rg4
17.Nf5 Bxf5 18.Rxf5 Nd7 19.Raf1 Rhg8
20.g3 Qf8 21.Bb5 Qg7 22.Bxd7+ Kxd7
23.R1f3 Ke7 24.Nf1 Rf4 25.Ne3 Rxf3
26.Rxf3 Kd8 27.Qf2 Be7 28.Nf5 Qg5
29.Qxa7 Re8 30.Qe3 Bf8 31.a4 Kd7
32.a5 Ra8 33.Qxg5 fxg5 34.g4 c6
35.dxc6+ bxc6 36.Rd3+ Ke6 37.Rd1 c5
38.b5 c4 39.a6 f6 40.Rd5 Ba3 41.Kg2
Ra7 42.Ne3 Bb2 43.b6 Rxa6 44.Rb5 Ba3
45.Nxc4

1–0

King's Gambit Accepted – Muzio Gambit variation

The Kings Gambit is one of the openings that was regularly seen in the Romantic era of chess, a time when both players went all out for the attack at whatever cost. More recently this opening has made a welcome return at the highest levels, though it now tends to be played more positionally. Club players have always enjoyed the type of exciting positions that this opening produces and the following game, though from the Romantic era, is typical of what can happen even today.

POPERT, H–NN
London, 1841

1.e4 e5 2.f4 exf4 Black accepts the gambit pawn. This can often lead to very exciting games as both players go all out to mate the other's King.

3.Nf3 g5 4.Bc4 g4 5.0–0!? White decides to sacrifice a piece and begin his assault on the enemy King before Black gets his army into play.

5...gxf3 6.Qxf3 (See diagram 144.)

6...Qf6 Black takes immediate countermeasures and now threatens 7...Qd4+ followed by 8...Qxc4. (A daring way to deal with this sortie is to play 7.e5 Qxe5 8.Bxf7+ Kxf7 9.d4 Qxd4+ 10.Be3!)

7.d3 Nc6 8.Bxf4 Bh6 9.Bxc7 Qxf3 10.Rxf3 (See diagram 145.)

10...f6 11.Nc3 Ne5 12.Bxe5 fxe5 13.Nb5 Ke7 14.Raf1 With these moves, White doubles his Rooks and takes total control of the open f-file.

Diagram 144

Diagram 145

14...a6 15.Nc7 Rb8 16.Nd5+ Kd6
17.Rf6+ Nxf6 18.Rxf6+Kc5 19.b4+Kd4
20.c3# (See diagram 146.)

1–0

Ruy Lopez

The prime objective of the Ruy Lopez can be seen in the move 3.Bb5, attacking the Knight on c6, the defender of the pawn on e5. By this means White intends to keep Black under constant pressure, and gains an initiative that can last for many moves.

The following game was played in a junior championship in Germany in 1996.

MUELLER, F (1615)–KRUSE, R

1.e4 e5 2.Nf3 Nc6 3.Bb5 Bc5 Black has elected to respond with the Classical Defence.

4.c3 (See diagram 147.)

4...a6 5.Bxc6 bxc6 6.Nxe5 Nf6 7.d4
White has gladly exchanged his white-squared Bishop for Black's c6 Knight. This exchange has netted White the e5 pawn and damaged Black's pawn structure. What is more, White has gained a powerful hold in the centre. (See diagram 148.)

Diagram 146

Diagram 147

Diagram 148

7...Bb6 8.Bg5 And now White pressures the other black Knight.

8...0–0 9.Nd2 Bb7 10.Ng4 Putting even more pressure on the remaining black Knight.

10...d5 11.e5 Bc8 12.Bxf6 (See diagram 149.)

12...Qe8 Not, of course, 12...gxf6, for White would reply 13.Nxf6+, and after Kh8 14.Qh5, and checkmate would occur on h7.

13.Nh6+ Kh8 14.Qh5 Qe6 15.0–0–0 gxf6 16.Rde1 Bd7 17.Nf3 Rae8 18.exf6 Qxf6 19.Ne5 Re7 20.Re3 Qf4 21.Kb1 Be6 22.Rg3 f6 23.Ng6+ hxg6 24.Nf7++ (See diagram 150.)

In the final position the black King is checked twice (double check, see page 23), both by the Knight on f7 and by the Queen on h5. This forces Black to move his King to g7, whereupon White will checkmate with Qxg6+ and Qg7#.

1–0

QUEEN-PAWN OPENINGS
(CLOSED GAMES)

The openings we have looked at so far have started 1.e4 e5 are are called 'open' games. Now we will look at several openings beginning 1.d4 d5. These are 'closed' games.

Colle System

We start with the Colle System, popularized by the Belgian Master, Edgard Colle. It is ideal for a novice, although it is played at the highest levels. Its main benefits for a beginner or strong amateur are that it can be played against almost anything Black dreams up. This game was played in the third round of the Norwegian Championships of 2000, between two players of master strength.

ROLVAAG, M (2260)–FOSSAN, P (2327)

1.d4 c5 2.e3 e6 3.Nf3 Nf6 4.Bd3 d5 5.c3 White's first five moves are the basis of the Colle, a deceptively quiet opening that often leads to fireworks. White's main aim here is to build up a solid and safe centre; then, and only then, he will attack Black along the b1–h7 diagonal. (See diagram 151.)

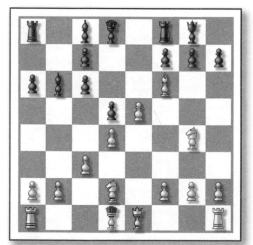

Diagram 149

Diagram 150

5...Nc6 6.Nbd2 Bd6 7.0–0 0–0 8.dxc5
This is an important move in preparation for
playing e4.

**8...Bxc5 9.e4 Qc7 10.Qe2 Re8 11.e5 Nd7
12.Nb3 Bf8 13.Bxh7+!** The first explosion
– a well-known combination known as the
Greek Gift sacrifice. (See diagram 152.)

13...Kxh7 14.Ng5+ Kg6 If instead 14...Kg8
15.Qh5 will soon win for White.

15.f4 Further preparation to trap Black's
King. (See diagram 153.)

15...Ndxe5 This is just desperation.

16.fxe5 Qxe5 17.Qg4 f5 The only move
that can delay matters.

**18.Qh4 Qe2 19.Qh7+Kf6 20.Nh3 Be7
21.Nf4 Qg4 22.h3** Black's Queen is
completely surrounded and lost. If 22...Qg5,
23.Nxd5+ exd5 24.Bxg5+ will follow and
White's attack will continue unabated. (See
diagram 154.)

1–0

Diagram 152

Diagram 153

Diagram 151

Diagram 154

The Colle-Zukertort

This is a version of the Colle System developed by the Swiss master, Zukertort, who, in 1886, lost the first official battle for the World Championship title to Wilhelm Steinitz. The following game is an example of the Colle-Zukertort.

FILATOV, L (2293)–MAYER, S (2222)
Philadelphia, 2 July 2000

1.d4 d5 2.Nf3 Nf6 3.e3 e6 4.Bd3 c5 5.b3 In this version of the Colle, White prefers to activate his black-squared Bishop (so do I!) rather than set up a strong pawn formation, as would be the case if the standard Colle System were being used. (See diagram 155.)

5...Be7 6.Bb2 Nbd7 7.Nbd2 b6 8.0–0 Bb7 9.Qe2 0–0 10.Ne5 Qc7 11.a3 a6 12.f4 This sequence of moves firmly establishes White's Knight on the 'outpost' on e5. From here the Knight looks menacingly into Black's position. (See diagram 156.)

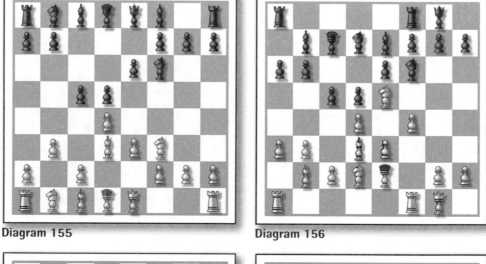

Diagram 155

Diagram 156

Diagram 157

Diagram 158

12...b5 As the centre is closed Black attempts to take countermeasures on White's Queen's flank.

13.Nxd7 Nxd7 14.dxc5 Nxc5 15.Bxh7+! Here's that wonderful sacrifice again ... or is it? (See diagram 157.)

15...Kxh7 16.Qh5+ Kg8 17.Bxg7!! A double Bishop sacrifice, an idea first introduced by the eventual second World Champion, Emmanuel Lasker.

The threat is simply Qh8#. Black's next move is forced. (See diagram 158.)

17...Kxg7 18.Qg4+ After Kh8 White will play Rf3 and then Rh3#.

1–0

Another wonderful sacrificial combination, but one that usually only works when the attacker can bring a Rook rapidly on to either the g- or h-files to effect checkmate.

The London System

This opening gets its name from the London tournament of 1922 where this set-up was regularly employed with much success. It is ideal for club players and those with little time for study in that it can be employed against almost any Black defence. The London System is still played at the very highest level and has recently been used by Vishy Anand, the world number 3, and Judit Polgar, the top woman in the world and accomplished Grandmaster.

AKIMOV, K–KOOLMEISTER
Riga, 1968

1.d4 Nf6 2.Nf3 d5 3.Bf4 e6 4.e3 c6 5.Bd3 Nbd7 6.Nbd2 c5 7.c3 Diagram 159 shows the basic starting position of the London System. White's pawn formation is the same as the Colle, the pawns on e3 and c3 giving strong support to the d4 pawn. The main difference is that White's black-squared Bishop is in front of the pawn chain, on f5, controlling the black squares in Black's territory.

7...a6 8.Ne5 Be7 9.0–0 0–0 10.Qf3 White prepares to launch a violent Kingside attack.

10...Ne8 11.Qh3 f5 Blocking off the white Bishop's access to h7.

12.g4 Nxe5 13.Bxe5 g6 14.gxf5 exf5 15.f4 Providing further support for the Bishop's outpost.

15...Nf6 16.Bxf6 Rxf6 17.Nf3 Rf7

18.Ne5 Now the Knight occupies the outpost instead.

Diagram 159

Openings

Diagram 160

Diagram 161

18...Rg7 (See diagram 160.)

19.Kh1 Preparing to bring the Rooks to the g-file to aid in the attack.

19...b5 20.Be2 Qc7 21.a4 bxa4 22.Rxa4 Qb6 23.Bf3 Be6 24.Qg2 Rd8 25.Rfa1
A change of plan brought about by Black's last few moves. Never be afraid to change plans if circumstances demand it, but don't change just because you see another attractive idea.

25...Rd6 26.dxc5 Qxc5 27.Rxa6 Qxe3 28.Rxd6 Bxd6 29.Bxd5 Qxf4 30.Bxe6+ Kf8 31.Nf3 Re7 32.Nd4 Kg7 33.Rf1 Qe5 34.Nxf5+ The pawn on g5 is pinned to the black King and cannot capture the invading Knight. Next 35.Qxe4 and Black's material deficit will be too large to offer a challenge to White's rampant army.

1–0

The Queen's Gambit
Here White's objective is to secure the centre. It mirrors the idea in 1.e4 (King–pawn) openings. In both King- and Queen-pawn openings, White aims to establish pawns on e4 and d4.

PILLSBURY, H–WOLF, H
Monte Carlo Monte Carlo (1), 1903

1.d4 d5 2.c4 A similar idea to f4 in the King's Gambit. In both cases White endeavours to put pressure on Black's centre from the start. If Black accepts the gambit pawn White will soon be able to play e4 and create a strong centre. (See diagram 161.)

2...e6 By supporting his d5 pawn with e6 Black means to make d5 a strong point.

3.Nc3 Nf6 4.Bg5 Putting pressure on one of the d5 defenders.

4...Nbd7 5.Nf3 Be7 6.e3 0–0 7.Rc1 b6
One of the problems for Black in the Queen's Gambit is where to place the white-squared Bishop; 7...b6 is one attempt at resolving this issue.

Diagram 162

Diagram 163

8.cxd5 exd5 9.Ne5 Now the Knight intends to invade via c6.

9...Bb7 10.f4 a6 As with the King's Gambit, White has succeeded in prising open a file for his own advantage – in this case the c-file. White was threatening Nb5 followed by Nc7.

11.Bd3 c5 12.0–0 c4 Now that the centre is closed Black attempts to counterattack on the Queen's wing.

13.Bf5 b5 14.Rf3 Re8 15.Rh3 (See diagram 162.)

15...g6 16.Bb1 Nxe5 17.fxe5 By exchanging Knights on e5 Black attempts to reduce White's attacking chances and give himself more room to manoeuvre. This is a standard ploy when you are under attack.

17...Nd7 18.Bxe7 Rxe7 19.Qf3 Nf8 20.Rf1 White increases the pressure along the f-file. (See diagram 163.)

20...Qd7 21.Qf6 b4 While this move is understandable, having been under such

pressure for so long, it allows White to invade via c5, a beautiful outpost for a Knight.

22.Na4 Qc7 23.Nc5 Bc8 24.Rh6 a5 25.Rf4 Rb8 26.Bxg6! Rb6 If 26...Nxg6, then 27.Rxg6+ fxg6 28.Qf8#. If 26...Nxg6, there follows 27.Rxg6+ hxg6 28.Rh4, and mates on h8, If 26.hxg6, 27.Rh8#.

27.Qxb6! Nxg6 If 27...Qxb6, White plays 28.Bxh7+ (discovering an attack on the now unguarded black Queen) and after 28...Nxh7 29.Rxb6, White will have a winning material advantage.

28.Qf6 Re8 29.Rf1 Be6 30.Qg5 Kh8 31.Qh5 Nf8 32.Nxe6 Rxe6 33.Rxe6 Black resigns, because if 33...fxe6 34.Rxf8+ and if 33...Nxe6 34.Rxf7, threatening Black's Queen and mate on h7.

1–0

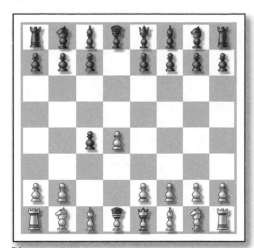

Diagram 164

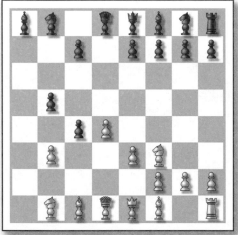

Diagram 165

Diagram 166

Queen's Gambit Accepted

The prime reason for Black accepting the gambit is to obtain freer action for his pieces. This may turn out to be a slightly riskier form of defence than declining the proffered pawn, but will probably suit someone with a more cavalier style of play.

SZABO, L–KELLNER
Schlechter mem Vienna, 1947

1.d4 d5 2.c4 dxc4 The defining moment. (See diagram 164.)

3.Nf3 There is no hurry to regain the pawn.

3...a6 4.e3 b5 5.a4 Bb7 6.axb5 axb5 7.Rxa8 Bxa8 8.b3 Endeavouring to hang on to his ill-gotten gains has not turned out well for Black. (See diagram 165.)

8...e6 9.bxc4 bxc4 10.Ne5 c5 11.Qa4+ Bc6 12.Nxc6 Qd7 13.Qa8 (See diagram 166.)

At best Black will remain a piece down, with his King stuck awkwardly in the centre, while White calmly brings out the rest of his army for the final onslaught.

1–0

The Trompovsky Attack

This is a relatively new idea popularized by the British Grandmaster, Julian Hodgson.

GELFAND, B (2685)–ROZENTALIS, E (2590)
Rapidplay15 Tilburg (5), 1992

1.d4 Nf62.Bg5 The start of the Tromp. White immediately puts pressure on the f6 Knight and, indirectly, the centre. (See diagram 167.)

2...e6 3.e4 h6 4.Bxf6 Qxf6 5.Nc3 g6 6.Qd2 Bg7 7.0–0–0 0–0 8.f4 White has already managed to gain an impressive centre for himself.

8...d6 9.Nf3 b6 10.h4 The centre of the board is won; time to attack on the wing. (See diagram 168.)

10...h5 11.e5 Qe7 12.Bd3 Bb7 13.Ne4 Nd7 14.Nfg5 dxe5 15.fxe5 White has now gained a half-open f-file, making possible invasion of Black's position via f6. (See diagram 169.)

15...c5 Black correctly attacks the base of White's central pawn chain.

16.c3 cxd4 17.cxd4 Rad8 18.Kb1 Nb8 The intention behind this move is to reroute the Knight to c6, so as to be able to put pressure on White's d4.

19.Nd6 Here White gains an important outpost. From here the Knight eyes important squares in Black's domain, notably e8 and f7, as well as attacking the Bishop on b7. (See diagram 170.)

Diagram 168

Diagram 169

Diagram 167

Diagram 170

19...Rxd6 Black decides he cannot leave the Knight on d6 and makes a small material concession. The game now enters the middlegame, so I give you the remainder without comment. Suffice it to say that White has gained a clear advantage from the opening. Although Black still has some counter-chances, a Rook versus a Knight and pawn should be good enough for a strong player to convert to victory.

20.exd6 Qxd6 21.Be4 Bxe4+ 22.Nxe4 Qd5 23.Nc3 Qf5+ 24.Qc2 Qg4 25.d5 e5 26.d6 Nc6 27.Qe4 Qxe4+ 28.Nxe4 Nd4 29.Rc1 Rd8 30.Rc7 f5 31.Ng5 Rxd6 32.Rxa7 e4 33.Rc1 Rd8 34.Rac7 Bf6 35.Nf7 Re8 36.Rd7 Ne6 37.Nd6 Rd8 38.Rxd8+ Bxd8 39.Rc6 Nf8 40.g3 e3 41.Kc2 f4 42.gxf4 Ne6 43.Rc8 Kg7 44.Kd3 Be7 45.Ne4 Nxf4+ 46.Kxe3 Ng2+ 47.Kf2 Nxh4 48.Rb8 Nf5 49.Rxb6 g5 50.a4 g4 51.a5 h4 52.a6 h3 53.a7 g3+ 54.Nxg3 Bc5+ 55.Kf3 Nd4+ 56.Kg4 Bxb6 57.a8 Qh2 58.Qb7+

1–0

TO SUMMARIZE

There are plenty of other opening systems apart from those we've looked at, but you now have sixteen possible openings to choose from, ten beginning 1.e4 and six beginning 1.d4. Each has many other lines of play for both the White and Black players. It will take time for you to decide what style of player you are and whether you prefer 1.e4 or 1.d4. The only way to learn an opening system is to play it.

OPENINGS FOR BLACK

DEFENCES AGAINST 1.e4

It probably isn't apparent just yet but it's a definite advantage to have the white pieces. Even at the highest levels of chess White wins about 56 per cent of games when starting 1.d4 and 54 per cent of games when starting 1.e4. The reason for the slight disparity between the two is the strength of the Sicilian Defence, which continues to get good results against 1.e4. Therefore it makes sense to start this section with a few variations of this defence (for more examples see Common opening traps, pages 98–109).

Sicilian Defence – Dragon variation

PIACENTINI, C–AHN, M
Belgian Championship, 1992

1.e4 c5 (See diagram 171.)

If Black replies to 1.e4 with e5 White can immediately harass Black's pawn on e5 with 2.Nf3 and can continue to maintain the

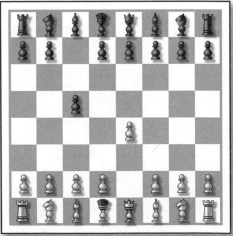

Diagram 171

initiative for quite some time. However, by replying 1...c5 Black still attacks the central square d4 and White cannot attack the c-pawn.

2.Nf3 d6 3.d4 cxd4 4.Nxd4 Although, by this means, White removes the pressure on his d4 square, Black now has a two-to-one pawn majority in the centre and has the use of the half-open c-file. With his next move Black attacks White's e-pawn. He has managed to do this on only move 4! (See diagram 172.)

4...Nf6 5.Nc3 g6 This move signifies the beginning of the Dragon variation, so called because the pawn formation at this stage is supposed to resemble a dragon's tail. Black prepares to fianchetto (see Glossary page 186) his black-squared Bishop on to its longest diagonal, from where it will exert lasting pressure on White's Queenside.

6.Be3 Bg7 7.f3 White's last move supports the centre, prevents moves by Black such as Ng4 and prepares to advance his pawn to g4 as part of a pawn storm against Black's projected castled King's position.

7...0–0 8.Qd2 Nc6 9.Bc4 Bd7 10.0–0–0 This sets the stage for a fierce all-out battle, with no quarter being asked or given. You can rest assured that with the Sicilian Dragon you never get a boring game! White's basic strategy in this line, known as the Yugoslav Attack, is to storm Black's defences with his pawns, to open up the h-file and deliver checkmate with his Queen and Rook. Black, on the other hand, will raid the Queen's side with his pieces. He will willingly sacrifice material in order to get to the enemy King and get his pieces into a position where he can check.

10...Ne5 11.Bb3 Rc8 12.h4 Nc4 13.Bxc4 Rxc4 14.g4 Qa5 15.Kb1 Rfc8 16.h5 Rxc3! This first sacrifice is a fairly standard idea in the Sicilian, especially in this variation. Black shatters White's pawn structure to gain easy access to his target. White's Rooks are not a lot of use at this stage, as there are no files open yet. (See diagram 173.)

17.bxc3 Bxg4! The pawn on f3 is overloaded, trying to support both g4 and e4 at the same time.

Diagram 172

Diagram 173

18.hxg6 If 18.fxg4, there follows Nxe4 19.Qd3 Nc3+ 20.Kc1 Nxa2+ 21.Kb1 Nc3+ 22.Kc1 Nxd1 23.Rxd1 Rc3 24.Qe4 Ra3 (threatening 25.Ra1+ and 26.Qa3#) 25.Nb3 Bc3!! 26.Nxa5 Ra1#.

18...Bxf3 19.gxh7+ Kh8 20.Bh6 Bxh6 21.Qxh6 Nxe4 22.Rdg1 Nxc3+ 23.Kc1 Qa3+ 24.Kd2 Ne4+ 25.Ke1 Qc3+ 26.Kf1 Qa1+ The only defence is 27.Qc1, when 27...Qxc1 is checkmate, so White resigns.

0–1

In the above example Black got in first, but that isn't always the case. Nonetheless, Kasparov used the Dragon in a defence of his title versus the world number three, Vishy Anand, and the system remains popular with many other Grandmasters, including Chris Ward, an ex British Champion, and the Hungarian, Dorian Rogozenko.

There are very many other ways for Black to play the Sicilian Defence, each of which would require a book of its own to expound all the possible themes, but I offer you one other variation for you to experiment with. It's called the Kalashnikov.

Sicilian Defence – Kalashnikov variation

STILLGER, B (2310)–HORVATH, G (2275)
Budapest, 1996

1.e4c5 2.Nf3 Nc6 3.d4cxd4 4.Nxd4 e5 (See diagram 174.)

This is the Kalashnikov variation. Originally this idea was considered bad because it leaves Black's d-pawn backward and weak. The modern view, however, is that Black has adequate compensation for this weakness, the speedy development it makes possible often yielding a significant initiative.

5.Nb5 d6 6.c4 White's idea with this move is to control d5 and to prevent Black from freeing his game.

6...Be7 7.Be2 f5 8.N1c3 a6 9.Na3 Nf6 10.exf5 Bxf5 11.0–0 0–0 Diagram 175 tells its own story. Although White has managed to maintain his pressure along the d-file and has control of the square d5, Black's pieces are better developed and

Diagram 174

Diagram 175

coordinated and he is fully prepared to invade down the c- and f-files.

White's Knight on a3 is merely a spectator in the coming battle.

12.Nd5 Rc8 13.Be3 Nxd5 14.Qxd5+ Kh8 15.Rad1 Qe8 16.Qd2 Qg6 17.f3 d5 18.Bd3 e4 19.cxd5 Bb4 20.Qf2 Ne5 21.fxe4 Nxd3 22.Qxf5 If 22.Rxd3, then Bxe4, and Black wins a lot of material.

22...Rxf5 23.exf5 Qf6 24.Rxd3 Qxb2 25.Rb1 Qe2 26.Rdb3 Bxa3 (See diagram 176.)

Diagram 176

Next comes 27.Rc2 and White cannot defend the invasion along his second rank. White resigns.

0–1

Gambits for Black

If you are not comfortable playing the Sicilian Defence but don't want to face the Giucco Piano (see page 60) or the very fierce Fried Liver Attack (see page 63) then perhaps you might like to try one of the next two ideas: the Elephant Gambit or the Latvian Counter Gambit.

Diagram 177

Example 1: The Elephant Gambit
SNUVERINK, J–DEN DEKKER, W
Netherlands U18 Championship Nijmegen, 1992

1.e4 e5 2.Nf3 d5 Black makes a bold bid to disrupt White's centre. (See diagram 177.)

3.exd5 Bd6 4.Bc4 f5 Black stakes a claim for some important central squares himself.

5.d3 Nf6 6.Nc3 Bb4 7.Bd2 Nbd7 8.Qe2 Qe7 9.0–0 Bd6 10.Rfe1 b6 11.Bg5 (See diagram 178.)

Diagram 178

11...h6 12.Bd2 g5 Black makes his intention to storm White's barricades with a broad front of pawns very clear.

13.Bb5 0–0 14.Bc6 This appears to be a useful outpost, but, in reality, the Bishop is simply stranded and takes no further useful part in the game.

14...Rb8 15.Rad1 Re8 16.h4 g4 17.Nh2 Qg7 18.Nb5 a5 19.Nf1 f4 Every pawn advance cramps White's position still further. (See diagram 179.)

20.g3 f3 21.Qe3 Kh7 22.Bc3 Ba6 23.Nxd6 cxd6 24.Nd2 Re7 25.Ne4 Nxe4 26.Qxe4+ Qg6 27.Qe3 Nf6 28.b4 axb4 29.Bxb4 Nh5 30.Rb1 Rf7 31.Kh2 Nf4! 32.Qe4 If 32.gxf4, then exf4 33.Qe4 g3+, and the pawns force their way through to promotion.

32...Qxe4 By exchange of Queens White hopes to reduce the strength of the attack.

33.dxe4 Ng2 34.Red1 Nxh4! 35.gxh4 g3+ 36.Kxg3 If 36.fxg3, then f2, and Black will soon promote or win material.

36...Rg8+ 37.Kh3 Rg2 38.Rd2 Bc8+ Mate follows.

0–1

The White Bishop on c6 has not taken part in the battle for 23 moves!

Example 2: Latvian Counter Gambit
This is not an opening likely to be encountered at the highest levels of play but some Masters still essay it as a useful surprise weapon.

FOSSAN, P (2320)–EILERTSEN, J
Norwegian Championship, Randaberg, 1989

1.e4 e5 2.Nf3 f5 As in the King's Gambit for White, Black makes an immediate assault on his opponent's centre and intends to utilize the f-file to help his invasion of White's position. (See diagram 180.)

3.Nxe5 Qf6 4.d4 d6 5.Nc4 fxe4 6.Ne3 Qg6 7.Bc4 Nf6 8.0–0 c6 9.Bb3 d5 In fewer than 10 moves Black has built up an impressive-looking centre, has an advantage in space, has pawns controlling several

Diagram 179

Diagram 180

squares in White's territory, and has the use of the half-open f-file. (See diagram 181.)

10.c4 White seeks to undermine Black's pawn centre.

10...Bd6 While Black continues with his development and attack.

11.cxd5 Ng4 12.Nxg4 Bxg4 13.Qd2 h6 Played to prevent 14.Qg5.

14.Nc3 Bf3 15.g3 (See diagram 182.)

15...Qg4 Black invades the weakened white squares.

16.Bd1 0–0 17.Bxf3 exf3 18.Qe3 If Black now played 18...Qh3 White would reply 19.Qe6+ and force off the Queens, effectively ending Black's attacking prospects.

18...cxd5 19.Re1 Nc6 20.Qe6+ Qxe6 21.Rxe6 Rad8 22.Nxd5 Nxd4 23.Re4 Bc5 24.Ne3 The constant pressure from Black has meant that White has not been able to develop properly; half of his remaining army is still in the barracks.

24...Ne2+ 25.Kf1 Rd3 26.Rc4 Rfd8 And now Black threatens 27...Re1 28.Nxe1 Rxe1#.

27.Ke1 Bb6 28.b4 Bd4 (See diagram 183.)

If 29.Rb1, then Bc3+, and White is forced to give up his c4 Rook for Black's Bishop, and the mating threats will not have gone away. White resigns.

0–1

Diagram 181

Diagram 182

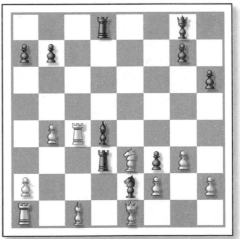

Diagram 183

Scandinavian Defence (Centre Counter)

The Scandinavian Defence is yet another way in which Black can respond to White's opening move of 1.e4. If you don't like the complexities involved in the Sicilian defence or aren't keen on the small risks that are involved in playing either the Elephant Gambit or the Latvian Counter Gambit then the Scandinavian Defence may be just the response you're looking for.

MINIERI, F–GIROLA, E
Lombardia, 1991

1.e4 d5 (See diagram 184.)

Black immediately attacks White's attempts at building up a strong pawn centre. Although some Grandmasters do not like this opening it is nevertheless still played at the highest levels of chess.

2.exd5 Qxd5 3.Nc3 Qa5 Bringing your Queen out early is generally considered to be unwise, but here, on a5, she cannot easily be attacked by the White forces. (See diagram 185.)

A standard position in this opening. After c6, a normal move in this variation, Black's Queen can return to c7 or d8.

4.Bc4 e6 5.Nf3 Nf6 6.0–0 Be7 7.d4 0–0 8.Ne5 Rd8 9.Bg5 Nbd7 10.Re1 Nxe5 11.Rxe5 Qb6 12.Be3 Bd6 13.Na4?
'A Knight on the rim is dim' is a useful saying to bear in mind until you become strong enough to know when it is safe to play your Knights to the edge of the board.

13...Qb4 14.b3 Bxe5 15.Bd2 Bxh2+! This type of move is known as a Zwischenzug, an in-between move. In this case it allows Black to harvest a pawn before moving his Queen from attack and relinquishing his Bishop.

16.Kxh2 Qd6+ 17.g3 Qxd4 18.Bd3 Qxf2+ 19.Kh1 b5 The Knight on the rim is attacked, giving Black time to develop his white-squared Bishop with deadly effect.

20.Nc3 Bb7+ 21.Ne4 Bxe4+ 22.Bxe4 Rxd2 The battle is effectively over. Black's invasion of White's second rank with his Rook and Queen makes White's defence untenable.

Diagram 184

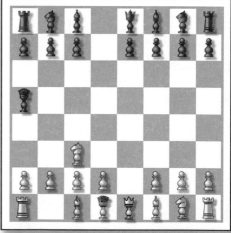

Diagram 185

23.Qxd2 Qxd2 24.Bxa8 Ng4 25.Bg2 Qh6+ 26.Kg1 Qh2+ 27.Kf1 Ne3+ (See diagram 186.)

The Bishop falls and, with the position being hopeless, White resigns.

0–1

Alekhine's Defence

Black's idea is to tempt White to advance his pawns so that Black can later destroy them.

STEINER, E–TARTAKOWER, S
Ujpest, 1934

1.e4 Nf6 2.e5 (See diagram 187.)

2...Nd5 3.c4 Nb6 4.d4 d6 5.f4 (See diagram 188.)

The aptly named four-pawns attack.

5...dxe5 6.fxe5 Bf5 7.Be3 c6 8.a3 e6 9.b4 Be7 (See diagram 189.)

The pawns look impressive but are vulnerable. Black has a good lead in development.

Diagram 187

Diagram 188

Diagram 186

Diagram 189

10.Nf3 f6 11.b5 Na5 12.Nbd2 0–0 13.Qc1 Nd7 14.exf6 Bxf6 15.Be2 Rc8 16.0–0 c5 Setting about White's pawns with gusto! Note that White cannot play 17.dxc5 because the d-pawn is pinned to the Rook on a1.

17.bxc6 White takes en passant.

17...Rxc6 18.Qe1 Nb6 19.Rc1 The pawns on c4 and d4 are 'hanging' and are ripe for attack.

19...Qe7 20.c5 Nd5 White's last move provided Black with this lovely outpost for his Knight.

21.Bb5 Rcc8 22.Rf2 Rfd8 23.h3 h6 24.g4 Bg6 25.Rg2 e5 This isolates the Black c-pawn.

26.dxe5 Bxe5 27.Bg5 Bf6 28.Qxe7 Bxe7 29.Bxe7 Nxe7 30.Ne5 Rd5 31.Re1 Black's next will be 31...Rcxc5, winning either the Bishop on b5 or the Knight on e5. White resigns.

0–1

This was a good example of hypermodern strategy at work: Black let White build up an impressive pawn centre, then proceeded to demolish it. Remember that pawns advanced too far, without proper preparation, will have to be defended, and this takes up other resources.

French Defence

The French Defence is played by several Grandmasters, including Victor Korchnoi, Nigel Short and Alexander Morozevitch and was the favourite defence of one-time world champion, Mikhail Botvinnik. It is a very solid opening, offering plenty of counterattacking chances for the player of the black pieces.

BRONSTEIN, D (2560)–UHLMANN, W (2555)
Tallinn (3), 1977

1.e4 e6 2.d4 d5 Here Black's strongpoint is d5. The only downside is the difficulty of developing the white-squared Bishop.

3.Nc3 Bb4 (See diagram 190.)

The Winawer variation

4.e5 Gaining space in Black's territory.

4...Ne7 5.a3 Bxc3+ 6.bxc3 c5 Though Black will remain weak on the black squares, he has, in return, weakened White's Queenside pawn structure and can now attack down the half-open c-file.

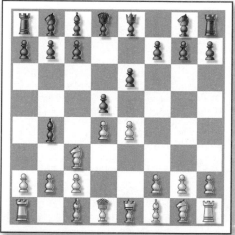

Diagram 190

7.Qg4 Qc7 8.Qxg7 Rg8 9.Qxh7 This is called the Poisoned Pawn variation, with good reason. For the sacrifice of a single pawn, Black now develops rapidly and gains activity for his pieces. White will not easily be able to get his King into safety but hopes to give Black problems with his passed h-pawn. The jury is still out on the merits of this variation.

9...cxd4 Black already threatens 10...Qxc3+, winning the Rook on a1.

10.Ne2 Nbc6 11.f4 With these moves, White is providing important support for the pawn on e5.

11...Bd7 12.Qd3 dxc3 13.h4 0-0-0 14.h5 Nf5 15.h6 Rg6 16.h7 Rh8 17.Rh3 d4 Although White has managed to advance his pawn to h7 his poorly developed army gives cause for concern.

18.Rb1 Be8 19.Qf3 Qd8 20.g4 Nh4 21.Qh1 Rxg4 22.Ng3 Rxh7 With the capture of this advanced pawn by Black's Rook White's hopes of securing any counterplay vanish.

23.Ne4 Nxe5! 24.fxe5 Bc6 25.Bd3 Kc7 26.Kf2 Rh5 27.Rf3 Qg8 28.Bf4 Nxf3 29.Qxh5 Rxf4 30.Qh6 Ng5+ This discovered attack on White's King will leave Black a Bishop and three pawns to the good at least; for example, 31.Kg3 Nxe4+ 32.Kxf4 Qg3#. White resigns.

0–1

Caro-Kann Defence

The Caro-Kann Defence was favoured by Anatoly Karpov, World Champion until his defeat by Garry Kasparov, the current world number 1. Like the French Defence, it is another sound opening, and it has the advantage over the French Defence of not causing Black difficulties with his white-squared Bishop.

HORVATH, J–CIGAN, S
Ravenna, 1983

1.e4 c6 (See diagram 191.)

2.d4 d5 3.e5 (See diagram 192.) Once again, as in the French, Black uses d5 as a strongpoint. 3.e5 is the Advance variation.

Diagram 191

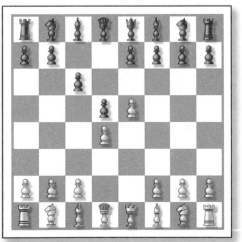

Diagram 192

A similar idea is often seen in the French Defence. White intends to cramp Black's position.

3...Bf5 4.Nc3 e6 5.g4 Bg6 6.Nge2 Ne7 7.Nf4 Nd7 8.Be3 Qb6 9.Qd2 h5! 10.gxh5 Bxh5 11.Nxh5 Rxh5 Black has already gained the free use of the h-file for his Rooks.

12.0–0–0 Nf5 13.Be2 Rh4 14.h3 Be7 15.Bg4 g6 16.Rhg1 0–0–0 17.Ne2 Rdh8 Black's two Rooks, operating in tandem, one behind the other, act together like a battering ram.

18.Nf4 Nh6 19.Nxg6!? White, possibly not liking the pressure Black is putting him under, elects to sacrifice a piece for three pawns.

19...fxg6 20.Bxe6 Nf5 21.Rxg6 Nxe3 22.Qxe3 Kd8 23.Bxd7 Kxd7 24.e6+ Kd8 25.Rg7 Qc7 26.Rdg1 Qf4 27.Rg8+ Rxg8 28.Rxg8+ Kc7 Although White still has three pawns for Black's Bishop, the pawns are weak and will soon fall. White resigns.

0–1

Philidor's Defence

This opening is not the best choice if you need to win, but it can be difficult for White to break down. It is not played much, however, at the highest level.

NOA, J–BLACKBURNE, J
Hamburg, 1885

1.e4 e5 2.Nf3 d6 (See diagram 193.)

The defining moment of Philidor's Defence. With this and subsequent moves Black makes e5 a strong point of his defence.

3.d4 Nd7 This strengthens the strongpoint.

4.Nc3 Be7 5.Be3 Ngf6 6.Bd3 Ng4 7.Qd2 Nxe3 Black sensibly removes White's black-squared Bishop and increases his own stranglehold on the black squares.

8.Qxe3 0–0 9.0–0–0 c6 This denyies White easy access to d5.

10.Rad1 Qc7 11.Ne2 Nf6 12.Ng3 Ng4 13.Qd2 Rd8 14.c3 Nh6 15.Bb1 Bg4 16.Qe3 f6 (See diagram 194.)

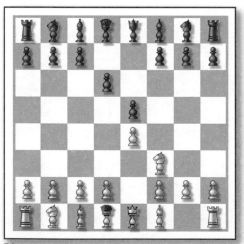

Diagram 193

Diagram 194

This strengthens e5 still further, especially as Black can now also play Nf7.

17.h3 Bxf3 18.Qxf3 g6 19.Bc2 Rf8 20.Bb3+ Kg7 21.Be6 Rae8 22.Rd3 Bd8 23.d5 cxd5 24.Bxd5 f5 Black has played a typical Philidor's Defence, slowly strengthening his position and risking nothing. Only now, when everything is secure, does English Master, Blackburne, nicknamed the 'Black Death', begin his advance.

The game continues.
25.Rfd1 Qe7 26.Qe2 Bb6 27.exf5 Nxf5 28.Ne4 Rd8 29.R1d2 h5 30.Qd1 h4 31.Qg4 Kh6 32.Bc4 Bc7 33.Qd1 a6 34.Re2 Ng7 35.Red2 Rf4 36.Bd5 Bb8 37.f3 Nh5 38.Kh2 Rff8 39.Qe1 Nf4 40.Re3 Ba7 41.Red3 g5 42.Rd1 Nxd3 43.Rxd3 Rf4 44.Kh1 b5 45.Qe2 Qc7 46.Qd1 Qe7 47.Bb3 Bb8 48.Nf2 Kg7 49.Ne4 Kh6 50.Qd2 Kg6 51.Bc2 Kg7 52.Bb3 Bc7 53.Qd1 Rff8 54.Qd2 Kg6 55.Bc2 Kh6 56.Nf2 Bb6 57.Ng4+ Kg7 58.Rd5 Rf4 59.Be4 Bc7 60.Qd3 Bb6 61.Kh2 Qf7 62.Bh7 Rxg4

0–1

Modern Defence
This and the Pirc, where Black plays an early Nf6, are closely allied systems. Black lures White's pawns forward with the intention of a sudden and violent counterattack later. The latter usually takes place down the Queen's wing.

MOSER, K (2315)–MOSKALENKO, V (2525)
St Ingbert, 1990

1.e4 g6 The defining move of the Modern Defence. (See diagram 195.)

2.d4 Bg7 3.Nc3 c6 4.Bc4 b5 5.Bb3 a5 6.a3 Ba6 7.Qf3 e6 8.e5 d5 9.exd6 Nf6 Black doesn't waste time in capturing the pawn on d6 – it won't run away!

10.Bg5 h6 11.Bh4 0–0 12.Nge2 g5 13.Bg3 b4 14.axb4 axb4 15.Na4 Nd5 (See diagram 196.) The Knight now occupies an important central square, from where it can move rapidly into attack or defence.

16.Rd1 Nd7 17.0–0 f5 Now there's a pawn storm on the King's wing.

Diagram 195

Diagram 196

Diagram 197

Diagram 198

Diagram 199

8.h3 h5 19.Bxd5 exd5 20.c4 Bxc4 21.b3 g4 If 22.Qe3, then Re8 23.Qd2 Bxe2 wins the Knight and one of White's Rooks. White resigns.

0–1

The advantage of using the Modern Defence is that it can be played against both 1.e4 and 1.d4. As can be seen from the above example, it is also very flexible, for, though Black usually attacks down the Queen's wing, when the opportunity presents itself, as here, Black can, just as easily, attack on the King's side of the board.

RESPONSES AGAINST 1.d4

Albin Counter Gambit

The Albin Counter Gambit, though not considered sound at the very highest levels of play, continues to gain good results against strong opposition. White in the game below has an Elo rating of 2225, not far below the rating needed to gain a FIDE Master title.

GIGERL, E (2225)–CIRABISI, F (2105) Caorle (3), 1988

1.d4 d5 2.c4 e5 (See diagram 197.)

3.dxe5 d4 Black immediately gains space in White's territory and creates some difficulties for the natural development of White's Queenside Knight.

4.Nf3 Nc6 5.g3 White's plan is to fianchetto (see Glossary page 186) his Bishop to g2 and advance his Queenside pawns.

5...Bf5 (See diagram 198.)

6.a3 Qd7 7.Nbd2 f6 (See diagram 199.)

8.exf6 Nxf6 9.Bg2 Bh3! This forces an early exchange of White's potentially dangerous Bishop.

10.0–0 h5 11.Re1 Bxg2 12.Kxg2 h4 This prises open the h-file.

13.e3 d3 14.Nxh4 g5 15.Nhf3 Qh3+ 16.Kg1 g4 17.Nh4 Ne5 (See diagram 200.) The earlier exchange of the g2 Bishop has left White severely weakened on the white squares around his King. Black now prepares to invade with his Knights.

18.f4 Rxh4! 19.gxh4 Nf3+ 20.Nxf3 gxf3 21.Qd2 Ne4 (See diagram 201.)

If the Queen moves, Black plays 22...Qg2#. White resigns.

0–1

The Albin Counter Gambit is well worth playing by those wanting to take their opponent out of well-known lines. I have used it myself for many years. Its only downside (as with the Budapest Counter Gambit that follows) is that if White plays 2.Nf3 Black will have to revert to something else.

Budapest Counter Gambit

RUBINSTEIN, A–VIDMAR, M
Berlin, 1918

1.d4 Nf6 2.c4 e5 3.dxe5 Ng4 (See diagram 202.)

4.Bf4 If White first defends the e-pawn with 4.Nf3 Black can respond 4...Bc5 and White is more or less obliged to play 5.e3, which hampers the development of his black-squared Bishop.

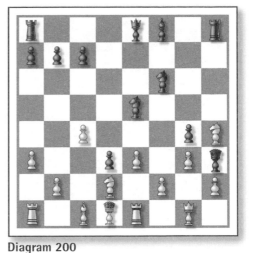

Diagram 200

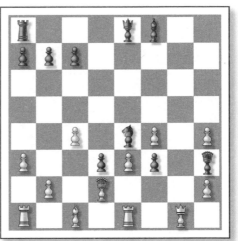

Diagram 201

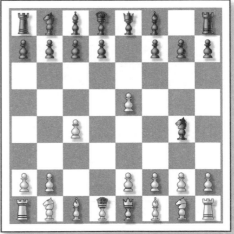

Diagram 202

Diagram 203

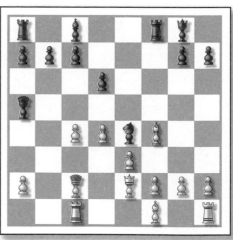

Diagram 204

4...Nc6 5.Nf3 Bb4+ 6.Nc3 Qe7 7.Qd5
(See diagram 203.) So far all of Black's
moves have been aimed at regaining his
gambit pawn, and White's at retaining it.

7...Bxc3+ 8.bxc3 Qa3 Black is threatening
to play Qxc3+, forking the White King and
Rook on a1.

**9.Rc1 f6 10.exf6 Nxf6 11.Qd2 d6
12.Nd4?** Rubinstein was a truly great
player, but here he commits an elementary
error: he moves a piece twice before moving
all his other pieces once.

12...0–0 13.e3 Nxd4! Vidmar, a very
strong amateur, takes advantage of White's
earlier error.

14.cxd4 Ne4 15.Qc2 Qa5+ 16.Ke2 (See
diagram 204.) There are no other really
safe squares.

16...Rxf4!! White's King is stuck in the
centre and neither his Bishop nor the
Rook on h1 can come quickly to his aid.
Vidmar's move exposes the White King to
a withering attack.

17.exf4 Bf5 18.Qb2 Re8 All of Black's
remaining four pieces are poised for the final
assault. White, on the other hand, can only
defend his King with a Queen and Rook, but
they are on the wrong side of the board.

**19.Kf3 Nd2+ 20.Kg3 Ne4+ 21.Kh4 Re6
22.Be2** Too late!

22...Rh6+ 23.Bh5 Rxh5+ 24.Kxh5 Bg6+
It is mate next move.

0–1

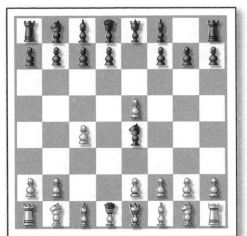

Diagram 205

Diagram 206

The Budapest Counter Gambit – Fajarowicz variation

BARLOW, M–DREYER, M (2345)
New Zealand Championship, Wanganui (3), 1994

1.d4 Nf6 2.c4 e5 (See diagram 205.)
Black's prime aim in this opening is to disrupt White's centre and launch an early assault on White's weak f2 square.

3.dxe5 Ne4 (See diagram 206.) This is the starting position for the Fajarowicz variation. Normally the Knight goes to g4, which is considered the sounder option.

4.Nf3 It is generally considered best for White to play 4.a3 to prevent Black's next move.

4...Bb4+ 5.Nbd2 Nc6 6.Qc2 d5 7.exd6 Bf5 The threat is Ng3, a discovered attack on the White Queen, which attacks White's Rook on h1 at the same time.

8.Qd1 Qxd6 9.a3 Bxd2+ 10.Bxd2 0–0–0
Black has five pieces developed to White's two. Virtually all of Black's army is prepared to begin the assault against the enemy King, still stuck on its starting square.

11.Be3 The white-squared Bishop and the Rook on h1 never see action.

11...Qe6 12.Qa4 Rhe8 13.Rd1 Rxd1+ 14.Kxd1 Nd6 15.Kc1 Nxc4 16.Nd4 Nxd4 17.Bxd4 Nb6 18.Bxb6 cxb6 19.e3 Kb8 20.Be2 Rc8+ 21.Kd2 Rc2+ 22.Ke1 Qd6
Black threatens 23...Qd2+ with mate to follow, as well as 23...Rc1+, which also wins.

23.Qf4 Rc1+ White resigns.

0–1

Diagram 207

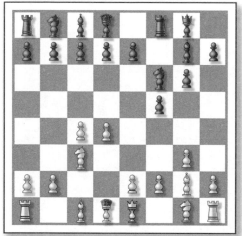

Diagram 208

Diagram 209

Dutch Defence – Leningrad variation

Black's aim in this variation of the Dutch Defence is a quick attack on White's castled King's position, usually by opening up the f-file and storming the enemy with pawns.

BROSIUS (2200)–DE LANGE, D (2290)
Berlin West, 1980

1.c4 g6 2.Nc3 Bg7 3.g3 f5 (See diagram 207.) By a slightly roundabout route we have reached the starting position for the Leningrad variation of the Dutch Defence. Normally Black plays f5 on his first move.

4.d4 Nf6 5.Bg2 0–0 (See diagram 208.)

6.Bf4 Nh5 7.Qd2 Nxf4 8.Qxf4 Nc6 9.d5 e5 10.dxe6 dxe6 11.Bxc6 bxc6 12.Nf3 Qe7 13.0–0 Ba6 14.Nd1 e5 The pawn storm begins.

15.Qc1 e4 16.Nd2 Rfd8 17.Nb3 Rab8 18.Ne3 Qe5 19.Rb1 Bc8 Having caused a little distraction on the Queen's wing the Bishop prepares to switch to the King's side of the board.

20.Qc2 f4 21.Nd1 Bh3 22.Re1 e3 23.c5 Rxd1! 24.exd1 exf2+ 25.Kxf2 Qe3+ 26.Ke1 f3 (See diagram 209.) The threat of f7+ with mate to follow is unstoppable.

0–1

Henning-Scharra Gambit

The Henning-Scharra Gambit is a very sharp counter gambit, sometimes used as a surprise weapon at Grandmaster level. Black concedes a pawn for rapid development and open lines. Openings like this, used only occasionally, can, however, upset the plans of even the strongest players.

PIRC, V—ALEKHINE, A
Bled, 1931

1.d4 d5 2.c4 e6 3.Nc3 c5 4.cxd5 cxd4
(See diagram 210.)

5.Qa4+ Bd7 6.Qxd4 exd5 7.Qxd5 Nc6
8.Bg5 Nf6 (See diagram 211.)

9.Qd2 h6 10.Bxf6 Qxf6 11.e3 0–0–0
12.0–0–0 (See diagram 212.) It's quite
unusual in this opening to find both players
castling Queenside (long).

12...Bg4 3.Nd5 Rxd5! 14.Qxd5 Ba3!!
15.Qb3 Bxd1 16.Qxa3 Qxf2 17.Qd3 Bg4
18.Nf3 Bxf3 19.Qf5+ Kb8 20.Qxf3 Qe1+
21.Kc2 Rc8 22.Qg3+ Hoping to exchange
Queens and relieve the pressure.

22...Ne5+ Blocking the check and
'discovering' one of his own.

23.Kb3 Qd1+ 24.Ka3 Rc5 (See diagram
213.) Black threatens to mate, starting with
Ra5+.

0–1

Diagram 211

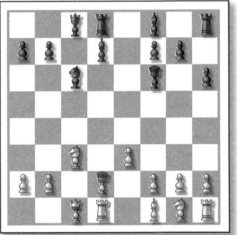

Diagram 212

Diagram 210

Diagram 213

COMMON OPENING TRAPS

The openings stages of a game are full of pitfalls just waiting for the unwary player. What seems to be an innocent, even good, move can lead you to all kinds of trouble. Your opponent could tempt you to play a move that looks promising but could lead to disaster. It would need a whole book on the subject to cover such pitfalls in depth, but this section highlights a few common traps in some of the openings we've looked at. Be on the alert for the opportunity to set them for your opponent, and take care that you don't fall victim yourself.

The 'Oh! My gosh!' trap

Possibly the most famous opening trap of all is this little gem, popularly known as the **'Oh! My gosh!'** trap.

MUHLOCK–KOSTICS
Cologne, 1912

1.e4 e5 2.Nf3 Nc6 3.Bc4 Nd5?! 4.Nxe5? (See diagram 214.) At this point cunning juniors cry out, 'Oh! My gosh!' as if they suddenly realize their 'error', and then play:

4...Qg5! 5.Nxf7 Qxg2 6.Rf1 Qxe4+ 7.Be2 Nf3# (See diagram 215.)

There are traps present in numerous chess openings. Some of them are rather obscure, requiring specialist knowledge, but a few of them occur over and over again and can occasionally catch out even relatively strong players.

Traps in the Sicilian Defence: The Morra Gambit

The Sicilian Defence (see under Openings for Black, pages 80–83) is the most popular opening reply to White's opening move of 1.e4. Black gets such good results with this opening, even when playing at the highest level of the game, that a whole chess industry has grown up to produce 'anti-Sicilian' openings.

At club level possibly the most popular of these ploys for White is the Morra Gambit – an opening that is well worth learning for all players.

The six sample games on the following pages should give you some idea of the many traps that Black can all-too easily fall into when playing against White's Morra Gambit.

Diagram 214

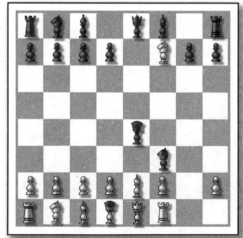

Diagram 215

Example 1
POULHEIM, K–NEUKUM, N
Erlangen (1), 1994

**1.e4 c5 2.d4 cxd4 3.c3 dxc3 4.Nxc3 Nc6
5.Nf3 d6 6.Bc4 Nf6?** (See diagram 216.)
This is a perfectly natural-looking move,
but in this case, for tactical reasons, it
is a mistake.

7.e5! (See diagram 217.)

7...Nxe5 8.Nxe5 dxe5 9.Bxf7+ The black
King is overloaded (see pages 52–53) trying
to defend its f7 square and its consort on d8.
The King is forced to capture the white
Bishop, as Kd7 would be check; now Black's
Queen is lost.

9...Kxf7 10.Qxd8 (See diagram 218.)

Black played on for another 15 moves before
resigning.

1–0

Example 2
In the following example of the Morra
Gambit, Black makes the same mistake as in
the previous game, but tries a different way
to get out of trouble.

ZIEMBINSKI, M–GAWLIKOWSKI, S
Polish Championship (Lodz), 1954

**1.e4 c5 2.d4 cxd4 3.c3 dxc3 4.Nxc3 Nc6
5.Nf3 d6 6.Bc4 Nf6? 7.e5! dxe5** Black
avoids the earlier disaster only to find
himself in a different pickle.

Diagram 216

Diagram 217

Diagram 218

8.Qxd8+ Nxd8 9.Nb5 (See diagram 219.)

If Black now plays 9...Kd7 to prevent 10.Nc7+ then 10.Ne5+ Ke811.Nc7#. One of my young girl pupils has won a serious game with this exact variation and defeated another very experienced teenager with the same line.

9...e6 10.Nc7+ Kd7 11.Nxa8 Bd6 12.Be3 Nc6 13.Bb5 b6 14.0–0–0 Nd5 15.Nxb6+ axb6 16.Bxb6 Bb7 17.Be3 Ke7 18.Rhe1 Ncb4 19.Kb1 Nxe3 20.Rxe3 f5 21.Nxe5 Bxg2 22.Rxd6 Kxd6 23.Nf7+ (See diagram 220.)

A Knight fork.
23...Kc5 24.Nxh8 Kxb5 25.a3 Nd5 26.Rxe6 White is the exchange up (having won a Rook for a Bishop) and has two connected passed pawns on the Queenside. These pawns are virtually unstoppable, so Black resigns.

1–0

Example 3
Black tries to find yet another way out of trouble.

KRNJOVSEK, A (2075)–RIZNAR, H
Kurent Ptuj, 1993

1.e4 c5 2.d4 cxd4 3.c3 dxc3 4.Nxc3 Nc6 5.Nf3 d6 6.Bc4 Nf6? It's that move again.

7.e5! Ng4 8.e6 Bxe6 9.Bxe6 fxe6 10.Ng5 Nf6 11.0–0 e5 In **diagram 221** Black attempts to deal with the mistake that he made on move 6. The problem with the resultant position, however, is that Black is exposed to invasion along the a2–g8 diagonal, his King remains in the centre and the remainder of his army cannot easily join the battle.

If instead 11...Qd7 then 12.Re1 e5 13.Qb3 Nd8 14.f4! – with advantage to White.

12.Qb3 White is already threatening to invade on f7.

12...d5 13.Rd1 Nd4 14.Qa4+ Nd7 15.Rxd4 exd4 16.Nxd5 e5 17.Ne6 Qc8

Diagram 219   **Diagram 220**

18.Nec7+ Kf7 19.Nxa8 Bd6 20.Bd2 Nc5 21.Qc4 Ne4 22.Ndc7+ Ke7 23.Bb4 Qd7 24.Re1 Nf6 25.Rxe5+ Black resigns. (See diagram 222.)

The Bishop on d6 is pinned to the King by the white Bishop on b4, so the Rook cannot be taken. Black will remain a Knight down and the onslaught continues unabated.

1–0

Example 4
Black tries a fourth way to untangle himself, but to no avail.

CIALDEA, A–DE BLASIO, A
Academia Cup Italy (2), 1996

1.e4 c5 2.d4 cxd4 3.c3 dxc3 4.Nxc3 Nc6 5.Nf3 d6 6.Bc4 Nf6? Here's that common error again.

7.e5! Nd7 A different way of trying to deal with White's attack.

8.Bxf7+! Kxf7 9.e6+ (See diagram 223.) If Black captures the White pawn with his King, White wins quickly: 10.Qd5+ Kf6 11.Ne4+ Kg6 12.Nh4#.

9...Ke8 10.exd7+ Bxd7 Although Black remains a pawn to the good he can no longer castle (his King has already moved) and White is better developed.

11.0–0 Bg4 12.Re1 White is sensibly placing the Rook on the half-open file.

12...Kd7 13.b4 Bxf3 By capturing the pawn on b4 with his Knight, Black only makes things worse by opening up the file to enable White to penetrate the black position with Rook to b1.

Diagram 221

Diagram 222

Diagram 223

Diagram 224

Diagram 225

14.Qxf3 Qb6 15.Qf5+ Kd8 16.a3 g6 17.Qg5 Qd4 18.Bb2 Qf6 In positions where you are at a material disadvantage, and especially when you are facing a fierce attack from your opponent, it is sensible to exchange (liquidate) pieces if at all possible. But White is having none of it and is out for conquest.

19.Qd5 Qf5 20.b5 Na5 21.Qd4 Rg8 22.Nd5 Bg7 23.Qe3 Qf7 24.Bxg7 Rxg7 25.Qc3 Nc6 26.bxc6 Qxd5 27.Qxg7 Black resigns.

1–0

Example 5
The Morra Gambit is a tricky little opening and has been used to beat many a strong player. Here's a different trap for you to watch out for.

GARCIA MENDEZ, B (1960)–MONTERDE PASTOR, A (1725)
San Jose (7), 1998

1.e4 c5 2.d4 cxd4 3.c3 dxc3 4.Nxc3 Nc6 5.Bc4 d6 6.Nf3 Bg4 (See diagram 224.)

This is an easy trap for the unwary to fall into, but it's one that you should be able to avoid if you just remember the dangers of leaving an unguarded piece (see page 102) – in this case the Bishop on g4.

7.Bxf7+ Kxf7 8.Ng5+ Ke8 9.Qxg4
Now White has regained his gambit pawn and Black's King is no longer safe.

9...Nf6 10.Qe6 Nd4 11.Qf7+ Kd7 12.0–0 h6 13.Rd1 hxg5 14.Rxd4 Qb6 15.Rd1 g6 16.e5 Ng4 17.Rxd6+ (See diagram 225.) The Queen, Black's most powerful piece, is lost. The Rook cannot be taken as the pawn on e7 is pinned to the King, preventing check by the White Queen.

1–0

Example 6
And now a Morra Gambit where it is Black who is setting the trap.

VOSS, A–BUERVENICH, S
Federal Republic of Germany-Girls Championship, Münster (4), 1990

1e4 c5 2.d4 cxd4 3.c3 dxc3 4.Nxc3 Nc6
5.Nf3 e6 6.Bc4 Qc7 Even though this is a
slightly unusual set-up, White continues
playing mechanically, no doubt following the
moves she's been taught.

7.Qe2 Nf6 8.0–0? 8.h3 was essential.
8...Ng4 (See diagram 226.)

9.h3 Nd4! This move is a clever idea,
which you would do well to bear in mind.
Not only does it attack White's Queen but it
also deflects the Knight on f3 from its job
of protecting the vital h2 square. (See
diagram 227.)

Diagram 226

White is already totally lost. The unthinking
manner of White's play has reaped what it
has sown. If White captures the Knight –
9.Nxd4 – threatening her Queen, Black
gleefully plays 9...Qh2#. If instead White tries
9.hxg4, then Nxe2+ wins the Queen. And,
finally, if White plays, say, 9.Qd1, there
follows Nf3+ 10.Qxf3 Qh2#.

This series of moves is known as the Siberian
Trap and was originally so successful – even
catching out a few a Masters – that it was
thought to be a possible refutation to the
difficult Morra Gambit.

Diagram 227

0–1

A trap in the French Defence
This a popular opening played at all levels
(for a fuller treatment of the opening, see
page 88). Black fights for control of the
square, d5.

NOLL, S–KUEDERLE, G
St Ingbert (7), 1991

1.e4 e6 (See diagram 228.)

Diagram 228

Diagram 229

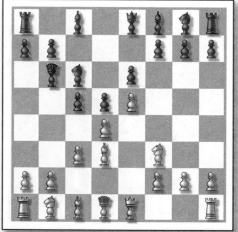

Diagram 230

Diagram 231

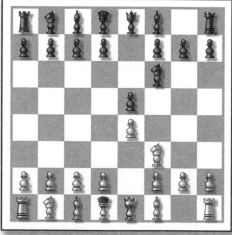

Diagram 232

2.d4 d5 3.e5 The Advance variation. White intends to cramp Black's position – the pawn on e5 attacks the squares f6 and d6 in Black's half of the board (thus gaining space). (See diagram 229.)

3...c5 Black, quite correctly, attacks the base of the pawn chain first.

4.c3 Nc6 5.Nf3 Qb6 6.Bd3!? The trap is baited! (See diagram 230.)

6...cxd4 cxd4 Nxd4 8.Nxd4 Qxd4 Black probably thinks he has won a pawn here, but, once more we have a piece, her Majesty herself, standing on an unguarded square. (See diagram 231.)

9.Bb5+! Oops – a discovered attack (see page 40). In this position the black Queen is lost.

1–0

A trap in the Petroff's Defence
Played at the highest levels of chess, this defence is usually employed when Black is seeking a draw.

Diagram 233

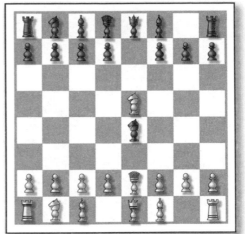

Diagram 234

1.e4 e5 2.Nf3 Nf6 This is the starting position for the Petroff's Defence. (See diagram 232.)

3.Nxe5 Nxe4? (See diagram 233.)

4.Qe2 And now White lines up his Queen on the same file as the enemy King. (See diagram 234.)

5...Nf6 The black Knight retreats ... (See diagram 235.)

...leaving the possibility of a discovered attack (see page 40) and check.

Diagram 235

6.Nc6+ (See diagram 236.)

This is not just a discovered check, but also an attack on the black Queen by the Knight. The Queen is lost and Black can take an early bath.

1–0

Diagram 236

Diagram 237

Diagram 238

Diagram 239

Diagram 240

A trap in the Englund Gambit

Here's a little trap you can set against 1.d4 specialists.

KRAUS, A–LUECKER, M
German-championships (U18) Germany, 1997

1.d4 e5 (See diagram 237.)

2.dxe5 Qe7 3.Nf3 Nc6 4.Bf4 The Bishop is placed on an unguarded square. (See diagram 238.)

4...Qb4+ This checks the white King and forks the Bishop on f4.

5.Bd2 Qxb2 6.Bc3 (See diagram 239.)
6...Bb4 Now he's pinning the Bishop on c3 and preventing Black from capturing the white Queen.

7.Qd2?? Bxc3 Now he's pinning the Queen on d2.

8.Qxc3 Qc1# (See diagram 240.)

0–1

I showed this trap to the Notts County Juniors just before the finals of the County Junior Championships. One of my pupils – a ten-year-old who played for the Notts team there – won with almost the exact set of moves shown above.

A trap in the Albin Counter Gambit

For more details on this opening, see pages 92–93).

PAVLOV, B (2200)–WILTON, G (2200)
Australia (4), 1973

1.d4 d5 2.c4 e5 (See diagram 241.)
3.dxe5 d4 4.e3? Bb4+ 5.Bd2 dxe3!
6.Bxb4 exf2+ 7.Ke2 The King is overloaded (see Tactical clues to look out for, pages 52–53), just as in the Morra Gambit shown earlier (see pages 98–103). It cannot protect both his Queen and the pawn on f2. (See diagram 242.)

7...fxg1(N)+ This is a perfect example of when to under-promote. Here Black promotes his valiant pawn to a Knight rather than to a Queen because the Knight gives immediate check to the King on e2 and White has no option but to deal with this. Otherwise White could play 8.Qd8+, followed by 9.Rxg1, and Black would be losing! (See diagram 243.)

8.Ke1 If, instead, White now plays 8.Rxb1, then Black replies Bg4+, skewering and winning White's Queen.

8...Qh4+ 9.Kd2 Not 9.g3, or Qe4+ would win the Rook on h1. Having indicated some more opening traps, I will run through the rest of this game without adding any extra comments.

Diagram 241

Diagram 242

Diagram 243

Diagram 244

Diagram 245

Diagram 246

9...Bg4 10.Qe1 Qg5+ 11.Qe3 Qd8+
12.Kc3 Nc6 13.Rxg1 Nxb4 14.Kxb4
Qe7+ 15.Kc3 0–0–0 16.h3 Bf5 17.g4
Bxb1 18.Rxb1 Kb8 19.Bg2 c6 20.Rbd1
Re8 21.Rge1 Nh6 22.Qf4 Ka8 23.g5 Ng8
24.h4 h6 25.Qf5 g6 26.Qd7 hxg5
27.hxg5 Kb8 28.Qd6+ Qc7 29.Qd7 Ne7
30.Qxc7+ Kxc7 31.e6 fxe6 32.Rxe6 Rh5
33.Re5 Nd5+

0–1

A trap in the Ruy Lopez

The Ruy Lopez is an opening named after
a Spanish priest, who wrote a work on it
in 1561.

LEVENS, D–THOMAS, A

The British Championship, Bath (Round 4),
1963

1.e4 e5 2.Nf3 Nc6 3.Bb5 (See diagram
244.)

3...Bc5 4.c3 f5 The Schliemann Defence
variation. (See diagram 245.)

**5.d4 exd4 6.cxd4 Bb4+ 7.Nc3 fxe4
8.Ng5 Nf6 9.d5 Ne7 10.Ne6** (See diagram
246.)

A sort of checkmate to the Queen! The pawn
on d7 is pinned to the black King by the
Lopez Bishop on b5. To make matters worse
the black Queen is trapped by its own army
and is therefore lost.

This was one of those happy occasions
when I knew the trap and my opponent
did not.

1–0

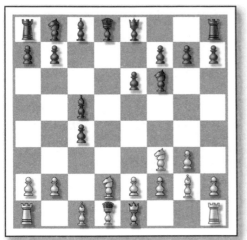

Diagram 247   **Diagram 248**

A trap in the Catalan System

Some suggested that my victory in the British Championship recorded above might have been the shortest in the history of the tournament, but that was far from being the truth. There have been many shorter, even at this relatively high standard, and the following is almost certainly the real claimant for the shortest game played in that tournament.

VEITCH–PENROSE
British Championship (Buxton) 1950

1.d4 Nf6 2.c4 e6 3.Nf3 d5 4.g3 dxc4
This is the position known as the Catalan System.

5.Nbd2 c5 6.dxc5 Bxc5 7.Bg2?? (See diagram 247)

Black's next move illustrates very clearly the weakness of the f2 square.

7...Bxf2+! Believe it or not, in this apparently innocuous position the white Queen is in fact lost. If 8.Kxf2, there follows Ng4+ 9.Ke1 Ne3 10.Qa4+ Bd7, and the

Queen has nowhere to run. If 11.Qa3 or Qb4, then 12.Nc2+ forks the King and Queen. And if, on move 9, White tries Kg1 instead, Black plays 9...Qb6+ and mates on f2. (See diagram 248.)

White, realizing the hopelessness of his position against possibly one of the strongest amateur players in the world, did the gentlemanly thing and resigned immediately.

0–1

TO SUMMARIZE

These few examples are only a taster of the countless traps that exist in chess openings. All are worth learning. If you would like to examine more chess traps then I'd recommend Steve Giddins' excellent book, *101 Opening Traps* (published by Gambit).

DEALING WITH OPENINGS YOU DON'T KNOW

Dealing with openings that you don't know is not easy even for the very best of players. In the case of Grandmasters, although they may know the main lines of just about every opening, there may be a few variations that have escaped them. In a tournament that was staged early in 2003, the world number 1, Garry Kasparov, played the Ruy Lopez, an extremely popular opening at the highest level. His opponent, another Grandmaster, responded with Bird's Defence. Although this defence is not generally considered to be one of the best responses to the Ruy Lopez opening, Kasparov was unfamiliar with its intricacies and in fact only just managed to obtain a draw.

Several years earlier, in a World Candidates tournament, Nigel Short faced his compatriot Jon Speelman. Speelman had learned of a new idea in a particular opening

Assessing the opening moves

With practice you will learn to recognize many of the common openings, but learning to assess what your opponent's opening moves mean about his overall strategy for the match is an important part of developing your skill as a chess player.

1.e4 White aims to control the d5 square and develop his Bishop somewhere along the diagonal f1–a6. It is too early to be sure about the optimum position for White's other pieces.

1...c5 Black will contest control of d4.

2.Nf3 White joins the battle for d4 while keeping an eye on e5.

2...d6 Contesting White's pressure on e5 and preparing to develop the white-squared Bishop along the diagonal c8–h3.

3.d4 Challenging Black's attempted control of d4.

3...cxd4 Although temporarily conceding d4 to White, Black has now gained the use of the half-open c-file.

4.Nxd4 Nf6 Black develops his Kingside Knight and attacks White's pawn on e4.

just twenty-four hours before they were due to play, and decided to try it out against Short in their vital match, and although Short was, and still is, one of the world's top players, he could not solve the new problems that were being set him over the board and duly lost.

How should you deal with an opening you haver never seen before? First, you should try as far as possible to follow the basic principles that are set out in the section Chess tactics (see pages 26–55).

Second, try to assess the main objective behind your opponent's opening and so his aim in the game.

As a novice player you may consider this beyond you, but every move has a purpose and if you are ever going to maximize your talent then you need to acquire this skill. Let me take you through the early stages of a well-known opening – the Dragon variation of the Sicilian Defence – to help you to understand the sort of approach that you will require.

5.Nc3 g6 Black clearly intends to fianchetto (see Glossary page 186) his black-squared Bishop; that is, to place it in this case on g7. Black clearly intends to dominate the a1–h8 diagonal, one of the two longest on the board.

6.Be3 Preparing to contest this diagonal.

6...Bg7 7.f3 This prevents Black playing his Knight to g4, attacking White's Bishop on e3. White may also use this to start a pawn storm against Black's King, as here it can support the move g4.

7...0–0 8.Qd2 White prepares to play Bh6, with a view to exchanging Black's now-powerful fianchettoed Bishop.

8...Nc6 Not only a sensible means of developing, but also a countermeasure to White's last move. If now 9.Bh6, then Bxh6 10.Qxh6 Nxd4, and Black wins a piece.

9.Bc4 Putting pressure on f7 and gaining control of the diagonal a2–g8.

9...Bd7 The only sensible square available to this Bishop, and it also allows Black's Rooks to unite together along the back rank or, later, to double up along the c-file.

10.0–0–0 White moves his King into safety while declaring his intentions to attack Black's Kingside.

10...Qa5 Preparing to attack White's Queenside.

There is much more to any opening than we've covered in this chapter, but studying the first ten moves of one opening (left) should show you that every move has a definite purpose. Gauge what the overall plans is then find a counter-plan.

A first-hand example

In the third round of a tournament, I faced a player who essayed the Nimzo-Larsen Attack against me. I had never faced this opening, while my opponent had been playing it for over twenty years. Although I was aware of the opening's main thrust, I did not know the 'book' lines and had to improvise.

JAMIESON, I–LEVENS, D
Dorset Congress 2003 (Round 3)

1.b3 d6 2.Bb2 e5 After White's first move it was obvious that he was going to fianchetto his black-squared Bishop, from where he would attack the black squares along the diagonal a1–h8. I had a choice, therefore, of contesting the black squares or attempting to control the white ones. I decided on the first course of action. By putting my pawns on d6 and e5 I aimed to construct a barrier against the pressure that would inevitably be exerted by my opponent's black-squared Bishop.

3.e3 Be6 4.d4 My opponent immediately tried to break down the barrier.

4...exd4 5.exd4 d5 This fixes Whites own pawn on d4 and effectively blocks up White's long diagonal.

6.Nf3 Bb5+ 7.c3 Just what I wanted.

7...Bd6 8.Bd3 Nd7 9.b4? This was intended to prevent Black expanding on the Queenside with b6 followed by c5, but succeeded only in restricting the range of White's own black-squared Bishop.

9...Ngf6 Getting on with the development of my army.

10.0–0 0–0 11.Nbd2 Bg4 12.Qc2 Bh5 13.Rae1 Re8 Contesting White's hoped for control of the e-file.

14.Rxe8+ Qe8 15.Re1 Qd8 16.Ne5 Bg6 The point of the manoeuvre Bg4–h5; now Black contests White's pressure along the diagonal b1–h7.

17.Nxg6 hxg6 It is generally considered better to capture towards the centre.

18.Nf3 c6 Reinforcing the pawn on d5 and preparing to play Qc7 to obtain my own pressure along the b8–h2 diagonal.

19.Bc1 Qc7 White, having got nothing out of his opening, offered a draw, which I accepted. My strategy seemed correct.

TO SUMMARIZE

The above approach, working out your opponent's line of strategy and devising your own counter, will work in most cases. However, if you are faced with a sharp tactical line you do not know, you will have to be great at concrete analysis.

THE
MIDDLEGAME

This section is mainly about middlegame themes, an important aspect of chess that has been touched on elsewhere in this book. In truth, it is too vast a subject to cover in one chapter, but there are certain elements within the Middegame that you would do well to learn.

So, where does the middlegame start? The easy answer is after the opening, but then, when does the opening end? The opening is that part of the game where each player is preparing for the battle, placing his or her pieces on ideal squares in readiness for the coming conflict.

KEY PRINCIPLES OF THE MIDDLEGAME

There is no clearly defined point at which the middlegame begins, but it is when both sides still have most of their pieces, with the Kings playing a passive role and each is kept as far out of the action as possible. The middlegame is the stage of the game where you need to be most creative and calculating, developing a firm plan of action.

The following examples should give you an idea of how to plan your own strategy.

GAINING THE CENTRE AND OPENING LINES OF ATTACK

The first game is 'The Evergreen', played between Adolf Anderssen, one of the greatest players of the nineteenth century and Jean Dufresne, who, although not one of the leading players of his day, wrote some influential chess books. The game reflects the style of the Romantic period of chess – an era when each player had a simple

strategy: to attack almost from the start, determined to checkmate the opposing King at the earliest opportunity.

ANDERSSEN, A–DUFRESNE, J
Berlin, 1852

1.e4 e5 2.Nf3 Nc6 3.Bc4 Bc5 4.b4
Diagram 249 shows an example of the Evans Gambit, a variation of the Giucco Piano. It gets its name from a seaman, Captain Evans, who first tried it out in about 1826–27 against a famous English player of the day, Alexander McDonnell. The idea behind the Evans Gambit is to open lines for White's pieces while at the same time gaining complete control of the centre of the board, a most important part of chess strategy. White's last move 4.b4 deflects Black's Bishop from the centre.

4...Bxb4 5.c3 This move attack's Black's Bishop and therefore gains time (a tempo, see Glossary page 190), another important aspect of playing chess. White can now get in 6.d4 and follow up with Qb3, so that his Queen and Bishop act as a battering ram against f7.

5...Ba5 6.d4 exd4 7.0–0 d3 8.Qb3 Qf6 9.e5 Qg6 10.Re1 Castling early, White gets his King safe and allowed his Rook to take part in the battle. The middlegame begins.

10...Nge7 11.Ba3b5?! 12.Qxb5 Rb8 13.Qa4 Bb6 14.Nbd2 Bb7 15.Ne4 Qf5 16.Bxd3 Qh5 17.Nf6+ gxf6 18.exf6 Rg8 Both players have potentially powerful attacks.

19.Rad1! Qxf3? 20.Rxe7+! Nxe7? 21.Qxd7+!! Kxd7 22.Bf5++ Ke8 If 22...Kc6, then 23.Bd7#.

23.Bd7+ Kf8 24.Bxe7# (See diagram 250.) White is a Queen and Rook behind, but has achieved his main objective: checkmating his opponent's King.

LESSONS FROM THIS GAME

- **White won the above battle because he controlled the centre from an early stage and opened lines for his own pieces to get at the enemy King.**
- **Black neglected to get his King into safety.**

The next element to look at is...

THE POWER OF CONNECTED PASSED PAWNS

MCDONNELL, A–DE LABOURDONNAIS, L
London, 1834

1.e4 c5 2.Nf3 Nc6 3.d4 cxd4 4.Nxd4 e5 We are now in the Sicilian Defence, Kalashnikov variation. (See diagram 251.)

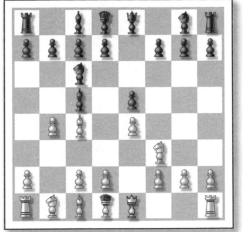

Diagram 249

Diagram 250

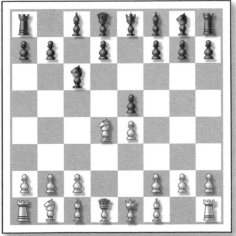

Diagram 251

Diagram 252

Diagram 253

Diagram 254

5.Nxc6?! bxc6 White's 5th move has simply served to strengthen Black's centre at his own expense. Black now has two centre pawns in comparison with White's one, and also has control of the square d5. (See diagram 252.)

6.Bc4 cNf67.Bg5 Be7 8.Qe2 d5 9.Bxf6 Bxf6 10.Bb3 0–0 11.0–0 a5 Although White has very sensibly got his King into safety by castling early he has clearly already lost the battle for control of the centre of the board. Black has already established pawns on two of the most important central squares, e5 and d5; the pawn on d5 is well supported by another pawn on c6; and both of these centre pawns control squares within White's territory: f4, e4, d4 and c4. (See diagram 253.)

12.exd5 cxd5 13.Rd1 d4 14.c4 Qb6 15.Bc2 Bb7 16.Nd2 Rae8 17.Ne4 Bd8 18.c5 Qc6 Black has placed his Queen and Bishop on the longest diagonal on the board, from where they hungrily eye White's vulnerable g2 square.

19.f3 Be7 20.Rac1 f5 21.Qc4+ Kh8 22.Ba4 Qh6 23.Bxe8 fxe4 Black has calculated correctly that his central pawn mass is more than a match for the loss of the exchange.

24.c6 exf3! 25.cxb7 allows a forced mate, starting 25...Qe3+.

25.Rc2 Qe3+ 26.Kh1 Bc8 27.Bd7 f2 28.Rf1 d3 The pawns advance like an unstoppable tide.

29.Rc3 Bxd7 30.cxd7 e4 31.Qc8 Bd8 32.Qc4 Qe1! 33.Rc1 d2 34.Qc5 Rg8 35.Rd1 e3 36.Qc3 Qxd1 37.Rxd1 e2 (See diagram 254.) What a pretty picture

Diagram 255

Diagram 256

Black has created, three pawns abreast on the seventh rank, all ready to promote. White sees the writing on the wall and resigns.

0–1

LESSONS FROM THIS GAME
- **Although pawns may be the lowliest unit in your army it is always worth remembering that they are potential Queens.**
- **A passed pawn – one that cannot be stopped by an opposition pawn – can be very dangerous indeed, especially if that pawn is well supported, as in the game just shown.**

DEVELOPMENT – GETTING YOUR ARMY OUT READY TO DO BATTLE

NAPOLEON I–GENERAL BERTRAND
St Helena, 1818

Not being a historian I am in no position to comment on Napoleon's skill as a general or military strategist, but in the following game his tactical insight on the chessboard is self-evident.

1.Nf3 Nc6 2.e4 e5 3.d4 Nxd4 4.Nxd4 exd4 5.Bc4 Bc5 By a roundabout way we have reached a kind of Scotch Gambit. (See diagram 255.)

6.c3 Qe7 7.0–0 Qe5 8.f4 dxc3+ (See diagram 256.) Take a careful look at this position. Black is trying to attack White's with just two pieces, while White calmly gets his King into safety and takes control of the centre. Chess is not like a James Bond film, where the hero single-handedly demolishes the entire enemy force. In real battles you need to get your entire army out of bed and on to the battlefield to have any chance of victory.

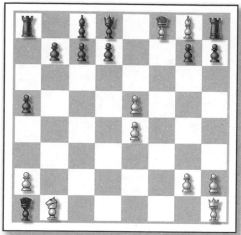

Diagram 257

9.Kh1 cxb2 10.Bxf7+! If 10...Kxf7?, then 11.fxe4+ K moves 12. Bxb2, and wins.

10...Kd8 11.fxe5 bxa1(Q) 12.Bxg8 Be7 If instead 12...Rg8, then 13.Qd5 forks the Bishop and Rook.

13.Qb3 a5 14.Rf8+! Bxf8 15.Bg5+ Be7 16.Bxe7+ Kxe7 17.Qf7+ Kd8 18.Qf8# (See diagram 257.)

1–0

LESSON FROM THIS GAME
- **After 18 moves Black still hasn't moved either of his Rooks nor his white-squared Bishop, and has paid the full penalty.**

OPEN FILES

SHORT, N (2660)–TIMMAN, J (2630)
Tilburg, 1991

1.e4 Nf6 2.e5 Nd5 Alekhine's Defence is a hypermodern system, an opening where Black voluntarily concedes the centre with the intention of undermining and taking control of it at a later stage. (See diagram 258.)

3.d4 d6 4.Nf3 g6 5.Bc4 Nb6 6.Bb3 Bg7 Black places his Bishop on the longest diagonal and begins to put pressure on White's centre pawns.

7.Qe2 Nc6 8.0-0 0-0 9.h3 (See diagram 259.)

The purpose of White's last move is to prevent Black playing 9.Bg4, pinning the Knight on f3 to White's Queen and adding indirect pressure to the pawns on d4 and e5. If Black were allowed to play Bg4, White could not recapture with his Knight because he would lose his Queen.

9...a5 10.a4 dxe5 11.dxe5 Nd4 12.Nxd4 Qxd4 13.Re1 e6? This could not have been an easy decision for Timman, but blocking in his white-squared Bishop like this and at the same time weakening the squares around his King (f6 is particularly weak) cannot be considered a Grandmasterly move. 13...Rd8 followed by Bd7–c6 seems to be a better alternative.

14.Nd2 Nd5 15.Nf3 Qc5 16.Qe4 Qb4 17.Bc4 Nb6 18.b3! Short, a very strong attacking player and the only Englishman to have challenged for the World title, considers his attack to be worth far more than his shattered Queenside pawns.

18...Nxc4 19.bxc4 Re8 The d-file is open (meaning that there are no pawns of either colour occupying it) so Short decides to make it his own.

20.Rd1 Qc5 21.Qh4 Short prepares to exchange Black's black-squared Bishop, while at the same time controlling the d8 square.

21...b6 22.Be3 Qc6 23.Bh6 Bh8 Exchanging Bishops would only serve to weaken the black squares around his King still further.

24.Rd8! Bb7 25.Rad1 Here the power of the Rooks controlling an open file can be clearly seen. Not only do they split Black's forces in half but they will soon dominate the seventh rank as well; this is one of the key ideas for gaining control of an open file. Note that Black cannot play 25...Rxd8 or there would follow 26.Rxd8+ Rxd8 27.Qxd8+ Qe8 28.Qxe8#.

25...Bg7 26.R8d7 One purpose behind controlling an open file is to penetrate to the seventh, or sometimes even to the sixth, rank.

26...Rf8 27.Bxg7 Kxg7 Now that this Bishop has been removed from the board, Black's black squares are not at all easy for him to defend.

28.R1d4 Rae8 29.Qf6+ Kg8 30.h4 h5 31.Kh2!! And now begins the most amazing King march ever seen, but this can only be undertaken because of White's dominance of the d-file and control of the black squares around the enemy King.

31...Rc8 32.Kg3 ce8 33.Kf4 Bc8 34.Kg5 Black resigns. White will next play his King to h6 and checkmate with his Queen on g7. If Black tries 34.Kh7, then Qxg6 leads to mate, the pawn on f7 being pinned.

1–0

LESSONS FROM THIS GAME
- **When you see an open file, or even a half-open one (a file with just one of your opponent's pawns occupying it), try and occupy it with your Rooks.**
- **If your opponent succeeds in getting his Rooks there first try to challenge them with your own.**

Diagram 258

Diagram 259

ATTACKING THE UNCASTLED KING

Example 1

TAL, M–TRINGOV, G
Amsterdam Interzonal, 1964

1.e4 g6 2.d4 Bg7 3.Nc3 d6 4.Nf3 c6 5.Bg5 Qb6 This is the Modern Defence, yet another hypermodern system. (See diagram 260.)

Tringov, who is an experienced Grandmaster, brings his Queen out early and goes pawn hunting. This is never a good decision against any strong player, but against someone like Tal, who is widely considered to be the best attacking player ever, it's just plain suicide!

6.Qd2 Qxb2 7.Rb1 Qa3 8.Bc4 Qa5 9.0–0 a6 11.Bf4 e5 (See diagram 261.) At this point in the proceedings Black has developed only his Queen, which has already moved four times, and one Bishop, while White has developed all of his army in readiness for the coming battle.

12.dxe5 dxe5 13.Qd6! This move ensures that the black King remains stuck in the centre of the board at the mercy of the white invaders. You need to remember that you cannot castle if this would involve moving your King *through* a square that would place you in check.

13...Qxc3 14.Red1 Threatening mate by 15.Qd8.

14...Nd7 15.Bxf7+ Kxf7 16.Ng5+ Ke8 17.Qe6+ Black resigns. If 17...Kd8, there follows 18.Nf7+ Kc7 19.Qd6#, and if 17...Ne7, then 18.Qf7+ Kd8 19.Ne6#.

Black has not had the chance to use either of his Rooks, nor his white-squared Bishop, and the Knight on g8 can only stave off mate by one move.

LESSON FROM THIS GAME

- **If your opponent is foolish enough to bring his Queen out early to go pawn hunting, let him do so and get on with your own development; it's the army you have on the battlefield that always counts, not the one left back at home in the barracks.**

Diagram 260

Diagram 261

Example 2

**LEVENS, D (LOUGHBOROUGH)–
HOGAN, P (LEICESTER)**
Chapman Cup, 1970

**1.e4 c5 2.Nf3 d6 3.d4 cxd4 4.Nxd4 Nf6
5.Nc3 a6 6.Bg5** (See diagram 262.)

6...e6 7.Qf3 (12f4 followed by Qf3 was
more commonly played here.)

**7...Be7 8.0–0–0 Qc7 9.Be2 Nbd7 10.Qg3
b5 11.Bf3 Bb7 12 Rc8 13.Rd2 b4!?**

Black has delayed castling, probably with
the idea of causing White to be unsure as
to which side to attack on. **14.Nd5!** (See
diagram 263.)

14...dxe5 15.exd5 Ne5 hoping to block the
dangerous open e-file.

16.Rxe5! dxe5 17.d6! Bxd6 If 17...Qxd6
18.Bxb7.

18.Nf5 Bf8? (18...Rd8!)

19.Bxb7 Rd8 And not 19...Qb7? 20.Qxe5+
Be7 21.Nd6+ wins the white Queen.

20.Rxd8+ Kxd8 If 20.Qxd8 Bc6+ wins
at once.

21. Bxa6 Black's poor development of his
pieces allows White to take time out to
grab another pawn, while still maintaining
his attack.

21...h6 22.Qd3+ Qd7 22.Qe4 This is
threatening 23.Qa8+ Kc7 24.Bxf6 gxf6
25.Qa7+ Kc6 26.Bb5+ wins Black's Queen.
Or 23...Kd8 24.Qb8+ Qd8 25.Qd8#.

23...Qa7 24.Qd5+ Kc7 25Qe5+ Kb6?

26.B3+

1–0

LESSON FROM THIS GAME
- **When your opponent has not yet
  castled, look for sacrifices that expose
  his king, keeping him off balance,
  before he has time to develop the
  remainder of his forces.**

Diagram 262

Diagram 263

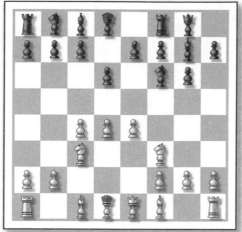

Diagram 264

Diagram 265

Diagram 266

ATTACKING THE CASTLED KING

Example 1

PIKET, J (2540)-KASPAROV, G (2775)
Tilburg,1989

Garry Kasparov is almost certainly the greatest player that has ever lived and his Elo rating, the number given in brackets after his name, is now over 2800, far higher than that achieved by any other player. The following game is a fine example of his attacking powers.

1.d4 Nf6 2.Nf3 g6 3.c4 Bg7 4.Nc3 0-0 5.e4 d6 The King's Indian Defence, one of Garry Kasparov's trademarks, involves storming White's Kingside with pawns. (See diagram 264.)

6.Be2 e5 7.0-0 Nc6 8.d5 Ne7 9.Ne1 Nd7 10.Be3 f5 After all that I have said about rapid development, it may seem odd that such a great player should have already moved both his Knights twice before developing his Queenside. But here, with the centre blocked (closed) for now and with his King safely castled, Black knows he is unlikely to be troubled by a rapid assault on his King.

11.f3 f4 12.Bf2 g5 Black's Kingside pawn storm begins.

13.b4 Because the centre is now fully closed the normal idea of counterattacking in the centre is just not possible, so White begins his own pawn onslaught on the opposite wing.

13...Nf6 14.c5 Ng6 15.cxd6 cxd6 16.Rc1 Here he is intending to penetrate down the open file.

16...Rf7 17.a4 Bf8 18.a5 Bd7 19.Nb5 g4
20.Nc7 g3 Black stakes everything on an
all-out attack on the opposite King.

21.Nxa8 Nh5 22.Kh1 gxf2 23.Rxf2
Ng3+! 24.Kg1 (See diagram 265.) Not
24.hxg3, or fxg3 25.Rf1 Qh4+ 25.Kg1 Qh2#
would follow.

24...Qxa8 25.Bc4 a6 26.Qd3 Qa7! 27.b5
axb5 28.Bxb5 Nh1! (See diagram 266.)

Black wins at least the exchange of pieces
and will be a piece up in the endgame, which
is a mere bagatelle for such a great Master
as Kasparov.

0-1

LESSONS FROM THIS GAME
- **Storming the opposition's castled
  position with pawns is a useful method
  of attack, but usually works best when
  your opponent has already moved one
  of the pawns that stand in front of
  his King.**
- **Before you begin a pawn storm always
  make sure that your centre is secure.**

Example 2

MARSHALL, F-BURN, A
Ostende, 1907

**1.d4 Nf6 2.Nf3 d6 3.Bf4 Nbd7 4.e3 g6
5.Bd3 Bg7 6.Nbd2** The opening shown
in diagram 267 is known as the London
System, after the tournament where it was
first popularized.

6...0-0 7.h4 Frank Marshall, the leading
American master of his day, begins an
immediate attack on his opponent's side of
the board; forcing open the h-file and the
diagonal b1-h7. The correct response to an
attack on the wing is a counterattack in the
centre, but here Black is too slow.

7...Re8 8.h5 Nxh5 9.Rxh5!? gxh5
Diagram 268

The above position is now ripe for a well-
known combination, called the Greek gift
sacrifice.

10.Bxh7+ Kxh7 11.Ng5+ Kg6 Not
11...Kg8? or 12.Qh5 wins.

Diagram 267

Diagram 268

2.Ndf3 e5 13.Nh4+ Kf6 14.Nh7+ Ke7
And not 14...Ke6? or play will continue
15.d5+ Ke7 16.Nf5#.

**15.Nf5+ Ke6 16.Nxg7+ Ke7 17.Nf5+
Ke6 18.d5+ Kxf5 19.Qxh5+ Ke4
20.0-0-0** Black resigns.

By opening lines for his pieces Marshall was
able to commence a typical King hunt,
forcing his Majesty, bit by bit, into the open,
where he would be finally checkmated. In the
end position White threatens 21.f3#, and if
Black tries 20...exf4 then White will reply
21.Rd4#.

LESSONS FROM THIS GAME
- **If your opponent attacks your flank,
  especially your Kingside, counterattack
  vigorously in the centre. Black failed to
  do this in the above game and paid the
  price, succumbing to a beautifully
  played Kingside attack.**
- **If the centre is secure then
  counterattack on the opposite wing.**

To summarize

To maximize your strategic skills there are many other lessons to learn, too
many for a book of this size, but, hopefully, these few important pointers will
give you a good start.

1   Plan to control the centre

2   Develop your pieces as rapidly as possible.

3   Always be aware of open files and half-open files.

4   Bishops and Rooks are long-range pieces and need open lines to operate
    effectively.

5   Passed pawns have a better than average chance of promotion.

6   If your opponent leaves his King in the centre, try to keep it there,
    so that your army can checkmate it.

7   Once your opponent has castled, look for ways to expose his King, often
    by storming his fortress with pawns; but first make sure that your centre
    is secure.

ENDGAMES

If it's hard to define where the middlegame starts it's harder still to say where it ends and the endgame starts. Even Grandmasters cannot agree upon the dividing line between the two. The US Grandmaster Larry Evans says that as a rule of thumb the endgame begins when the Queens are gone. However, this seems too imprecise to me and I would suggest that the defining moment is when the King is no longer a pampered royal, hidden and protected behind his subjects, but becomes instead a fighting unit that can enter the main arena to take his part in the final battle.

THE PLAYERS' AIMS DURING THE ENDGAME

All of chess's great players and champions have been experts at the endgame, so you can see that it is an important part of the game to master. One of the main aims during the endgame – the final phase of the game – is to reach the far side of the board with a pawn, thus allowing the player to promote it to a piece of higher value, which can often prove terminal to the opponent's game. Unlike in the rest of the game, the King can become an important offensive piece, especially when there are only Kings and pawns left on the board. When other pieces remain on the board, such as one Rook per side, the players have to maintain a balance between offence and defence.

TRANSITION TO THE ENDGAME

The example below demonstrates the fine line between middlegame and endgame as the Kings suddenly emerge onto the scene.

Wittke, C–Mandelkow, H
Berlin West, 1987

I would classify the position shown in diagram 269 as the late middlegame, and not just because the Queens are still on the board. Equally important, both Kings are exposed and could easily be mated if they attempted to move into the main battle arena.

35...Qe7 36.Qxe7 Bxe7 After these exchanges, however, the Kings begin to play a vital part in the proceedings, and thus, to my mind, this is where the endgame truly starts. (See diagram 270.)

37.Kf2 The white King heads towards the centre.

37...Rg5 38.Ra3 Kf6 The black King also moves into the main battle area.

39.Rg3 Rh5 40.Bd1 Rh1 41.Re3 Ke5 42.Kf3 Kd4 The black King is now right at the heart of the battle and plays a large part in this final phase, helping to push its c-pawn to promotion. (See diagram 271.)

43.Ra3 c3 44.Ra7 Bg5 45.Rb7 Re1 46.Rxb5 Re3+ 47.Kf2 Bh4+ 48.g3 Bxg3+ 49.Kg2 Be5 50.Rb7 Bh3+ 51.Kg1 In this position shown in diagram 272, without waiting for Black's reply, White resigned. Due to the black King advancing to d4 and cutting off the white King's means of escape, White will soon be mated (for example, 51...Re1+ 52.Kf2 Rf1+ 53.Ke2 Rf6, followed by Bg4+ and Bg3#.

0–1

Diagram 270

Diagram 271

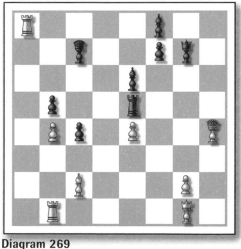

Diagram 269

Diagram 272

ELEMENTS OF THE ENDGAME

There are four key elements to the endgame: (1) Opposition; (2) Stalemate; (3) Zugzwang; and (4) Triangulation. I will deal with points (1), (3) and (4) below.

OPPOSITION

Understanding the concept of the opposition will help you to win many endgames, especially when there are only the two Kings and one or more pawns left on the board. The opposition occurs when there is an odd number of squares between the two Kings, whether this is laterally, vertically or diagonally. It is the player who does not have the next move who is described as having the opposition.

Example 1: Gaining the Opposition

In the following position it is Black's turn to move.

Diagram 273 shows black winning by gaining the opposition.

1...Kf3 Here he is forcing the white King to move.

2.Ke1 Kg2. By winning the opposition Black has gained control of the queening square, f1, and can now force home his pawn. If 2.Kg1 Black plays to the other side, 2...Ke2. Note that if 1...f3? White gains the opposition with 2.Ke1, and easily draws.

Example 2: Distant Opposition

The above example is a simple demonstration of the use of the opposition, but at times the Kings are separated by more than two squares. When they are separated by three or five squares but standing on the same file or rank they are described as being in distant opposition. Even gaining the distant opposition is helpful in winning or drawing King and pawn endgames.

The position shown in diagram 274 is taken from a game between the Yugoslav Grandmaster Svetozar Gligoric and the famous Bobby Fischer.

It is Fischer (Black), to play next, and he can move his King to any one of five squares. The correct square draws, all the others lose! Using his knowledge of the opposition Fischer correctly chose **1...Kb8!** Now, if White plays 2.Kd5 Black replies Kb7 (thus gaining the diagonal opposition); 2.Kc5

Diagram 273

Diagram 274

Diagram 275

Diagram 276

would be met by Kc7 (regaining the opposition); and 2.Kb5 is answered by Kb7, when, once again, Black retains the opposition and draws.

STALEMATE

As discussed earlier, stalemate occurs when a player is unable to make any move that would not result in check, and the game is thus draw. We have already explored this in the section Stalemate and other drawing mechanisms (see pages 32–34), but, as we shall see, stalemate possibilities abound in the endgame.

It is all too easy, despite having a winning advantage in terms of material, to let your struggling opponent off the hook by inadvertently stalemating them. On the other hand, there are times when you are in trouble yourself when you can save your bacon through engineering a stalemate yourself. Examples of various endgame stalemates are given throughout the rest of this section.

ZUGZWANG

This is best described as a position where the player whose turn it is to move would like to pass if that were possible. Instead, he or she is forced to make a detrimental move. In the position shown in diagram 275, whichever player is to move next is in Zugzwang, unable to avoid losing his pawn and with it the game.

In the position shown in diagram 276 Black is ahead by two pawns but White can effect a stunning Zugzwang which wins the game.

1.Rd1+ Rg8 2.Rf1!! Not, of course, 2.Rxg8+??, which would be met by hxg8=Q+. Black is in Zugzwang: every move he makes would mean he loses. If 2...Rxf8+ then 3.Kxf8 a5 4.bxa5, and the passed pawn wins the race to promote and announces checkmate a6–a7–a8=Q#.

TRIANGULATION

This is a method of regaining the same or similar position, only with your opponent to move instead of you. Like Zugzwang, it relates to advanced chess.

Example 1: Queen Triangulation

In the position shown in diagram 277 White cannot play 1.Qxa1 because it would be stalemate. What he needs to do is somehow engineer the same position but with Black's King on a8, so that Qxa1 would be check.

1.Qe8 Threatening 2.Ke7#.

1...Qa4 2.Qe5+ 3.Ka8 Qh8! Now Black cannot return to a1 because of Qxa1+ then Qa7#. White wins this game by an unusual Queen triangulation (Q–e8–e5–a8).

Example 2: King triangulation

The position shown in diagram 278 illustrates a more normal King triangulation.

To have a chance of winning this endgame White needs to recreate the same position, but with Black to move instead.

1.Ka3 Kb6 2.Kb2 Ka5 3.Kb3! By dancing around that small triangle, a3–b2–b3, White has achieved his objective. Black is now forced to play 3...Kb6 or Ka6 and now White can play Kc3–d3–e4 eventually winning Black's pawn.

AVOIDING DISASTER MOVES

This a subject that probably needs the help of a psychologist! Many articles have been written on it by players better qualified than I am. Even Grandmasters sometimes make inexplicable blunders. The world number three, Vishy Anand, once lost a match in seven moves and competitors in various World Championships have all had their share of disasters. Tiredness or shortage of time in a difficult position can both play a part, but sometimes there simply isn't an easy explanation.

The position shown in diagram 279 was taken from a game played in Ostend in Belgium in 1905 between two of the best Grandmasters of the day: Tchigorin (White) and Tarrasch (Black).

Thinking that his position was hopeless Tchigorin resigned, yet the position is in fact drawn! He missed 1.Kg4! Ke5 2.g6! h6 3.Kh5 Kxf5 – stalemate! Tchigorin overlooked the stalemate possibility and resigned prematurely.

Note that if instead Black plays 2...hxg6 3.fxg6 f5+ 4.Kg5 f4 5.h5 f3 6.h6 7.Kxh6 f2 8.g7 follows, and both sides queen.

Diagram 277

Diagram 278

Kasparov, probably the greatest player of all time, also resigned prematurely against the computer, Deep Blue, when he too had a drawn position.

I never mind losing against someone who has simply outplayed me, and I always try to learn something from such reverses, but when I have outplayed my opponent for two or three hours only to give the game away through a disaster move occasioned by a single lapse of concentration, I don't sleep well that night. The only advice I can give you is to look, look and look again. And, while you're still a novice, never resign.

Diagram 279

CHECKMATING THE KING WITH LIMITED MATERIAL

Checkmating the King with limited material refers to the basic mates of a lone King against (1) King and Queen, (2) King and two Rooks, (3) King and one Rook, (4) King and two Bishops, (5) King, Bishop and Knight.

In every case the technique is almost identical: the lone King is driven to a corner or one side of the board until he can run no further and the *coup de grâce* is delivered.

KING AND QUEEN AGAINST KING

The Position To Aim For

Diagrams 280 and 281 show the type of final position you need to aim for. Both, of course, are checkmate.

Diagram 280

Diagram 281

Diagram 282

Diagram 283

Diagram 284

Checkmate could also be made with a lone King in a corner, as shown in diagram 282

Although any of these positions is fairly easy to achieve you must beware of stalemating your opponent, resulting in a draw.

Diagrams 283 and 284 illustrate all too painfully what can happen when you are over-eager to trap your opponent's King.

The Checkmate Process

So, how do we get to a checkmate? The next diagram shows a possible starting position for a Queen and King against a King. Even though this is an easy checkmate to achieve, always remember the fifty-move rule when the last pawn has been removed: namely if fifty moves are made without a pawn move or a capture, then a draw may be claimed.

The first thing to do is to reduce the scope of the defending King. (See diagram 285.)

1.Qe4 (See diagram 286.) The black King has only 16 squares in which to operate.

1...Kc5 2.Kb2 Kb5 3.Kb3 Kc5 4.Qe5+ (See diagram 287.) The white King and

Diagram 285

Diagram 286

Diagram 287

Diagram 288

Diagram 289

Queen, by combining together, have reduced the defending King's range still further.

4...Kc6 5.Kc4 Kd7 6.Kc5 Kd8 7.Qg7 This last move consigns the black King to the back rank, and by placing your Queen far from the defending King you remove all likelihood of a stalemate. (See diagram 288.)

7...Kc8 8.Kc6 Your King closes in for the final act.

8...Kb8 9.Qb7#

KING AND TWO ROOKS AGAINST A LONE KING

This is the only checkmate with limited material where the attacking King is not needed. (See diagram 289.)

The Checkmate Process

Assuming a starting position as in the above diagram, White commences with...

1.Ra3 a move that neatly bars the lone black King from advancing any farther down the board.

Diagram 290

1...Kf4 2.Rh4+ Kg5 In diagram 290 the black King is forced to retreat because the second Rook acts as a barrier.

3.Rb4 Here he avoids capture.

3...Kf5 4.Ra5+ Ke6 5.Rb6+ Kd7 6.Ra7+ Kc8 7.Rh7 7.Rb8+ would allow the black King to capture the Rook.

7...Kd8 8.Rb8# In diagram 291 the two Rooks act as a team, alternately checking the opposing King and forcing it to the edge of the board, where checkmate is delivered.

KING AND ROOK AGAINST A LONE KING

With this checkmate, the King plays a vital part. (See diagram 292.)

The Checkmate Process

1.Kg7 Ke5 2.Kf7 f5 3.Re1 (See diagram 293.) By taking up the opposition to the defending King the black King is forced down the board.

Diagram 291

Diagram 292

Diagram 293

3...Kf4 4.Kf6 Kf3 5.Kf5 Kf2 6.Re4
(See diagram 294.) Now the defending King is limited to just nine squares.

6...Kf3 7.Ke5 Kf2 8.Kf4
White takes up the opposition once more.

8...Kf1 9.Kf3 Kg1 10.Rh4! (See diagram 295.) This last move forces the black King to where you want him, opposite your own King.

10...Kf1 11.Rh1#

KING AND TWO BISHOPS AGAINST A LONE KING
Although this checkmate is not too common it is well worth learning.

The Position To Aim For
Diagram 296 illustrates the final position to aim for.

Pitfalls
Diagram 297 shows, with Black to move, the position to avoid: stalemate.

Diagram 295

Diagram 296

Diagram 294

Diagram 297

Diagram 298

Diagram 299

Diagram 300

The Checkmate Process

If we start with the opposing King in the middle of the board, your first step is to bring your own King into the fray. (See diagram 298.)

1.Kb2 Ke4 2.Kc3 Kd5 3.Bf3+ Ke5 4.Bg3+ Ke6 (See diagram 299.) As with the two Rooks, the two Bishops, working in parallel to each other, act like an electric fence: nothing can cross their path in safety.

5.Kd4 Kf5 6.Kd5 Kf6 7.Bg4 Kg5 8.Bd7 Kf6 9.Bh4+ Kg6 10.Ke5 Kf7 11.Kf5 Kg7 12.Be8 Kf8 13.Bg6 Kg7 14.Be7 Kg8 And now a little tango, as the white King and the Bishop on g6 swap places.

15.Kf6 Kh8 16.Bf5 Kg8 17.Kg6 Kh8 (See diagram 300.)

18.Bd6 Kg8 19.Be6+ Kh8 20.Be5#

KING, KNIGHT AND BISHOP AGAINST A LONE KING

Although knowledge of this checkmate is part of the British Chess Federation's Certificate of Excellence awards scheme, Gold Standard, I will not dwell too much on it here. Not only is it a rare occurrence, but it is also advanced knowledge rather than basic chess. Very few serious chess players ever come across it.

The Position To Aim For

Diagrams 301 and 302 show the typical checkmate finishes using a Knight and Bishop, supported by the King. Note that the lone King has to be driven into a corner that is the same colour as your Bishop; in other words a white corner square for a white-squared Bishop and a black corner square for a black-squared Bishop. Driving the enemy

King in to a corner should not be too difficult, but remember that this checkmate, even with best play, takes around 35 moves to complete; so accuracy is vital. Normally the defending King will head for the opposite-coloured corner square to the colour of your Bishop. The diagram below assumes that this is what has happened in this case.

The Checkmate Process
1.Nf7+ Kg8 2.Bg6 A necessary waiting move. (See diagram 303.)

2...Kf8 3.Bh7 To prevent the black King returning to h8.

3...Ke8 4.Nd4 Kd8 5.Ke6 Kc7 Black now attempts to escape to a1.

6.Nd7 This part of the checkmate is well worth noting, even for a beginner: the Knight covers squares of the colour not covered by the Bishop.

6...Kc6 7.Bd3 Kc7 8.Bb5 Kd8 9.Kd6 Ke8 Heading back to h8.

10.Bc4 Imagine that the line between the f- and g-files is the edge of the board: we have reached a similar position to that with which we started this campaign.

10...Kd8 11.Bf7 Kc8 12.Nb5 Kg8 13.Kf3 Kh7 14.Kf7 Ka8 15.Kb6 Kb8 16.Be6 Kh8 17.Bd7 Kb8 18.Na6+ Ka8 19.Bc6# White could also finish off with the following:

17.Bc8 Kb8 18.Ba6 Ka8 19.Bb7+ Kb8 20.Nc6#

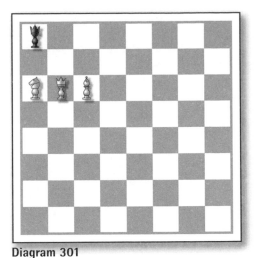

Diagram 301

Diagram 302

Diagram 303

Diagram 304

Diagram 305

KING AND TWO KNIGHTS AGAINST A LONE KING

It is impossible to force checkmate with this limited material but, oddly, it can be forced if the defending side also has a lone pawn. This is because with a pawn the lone King cannot be stalemated, and this gives the attacker more room for manoeuvre. However this checkmate is even rarer, and more difficult, than mating with a King, Knight and Bishop. Only a few years ago a leading Grandmaster, faced with such a situation, failed to find the correct solution. How to secure such a checkmate is illustrated in diagram 304

TRICKS, TRAPS AND FINESSES

Chess is such a complex and interesting game that it is, unsurprisingly, full of tricks, traps and finesses. As we have seen, there are numerous traps in the opening stages (see Common opening traps, pages 98–109) but they also occur in other stages of chess; especially endings. You can set them for an unwary opponent but if you're not careful you can find yourself caught in them as well.

PASSED PAWNS

Diagram 305 illustrates an easy win for White, if you know what to do.

1.g6! hxg6 2.f6! And wins. If 2...gxf6 you play 3.h6, and the pawn promotes. While if 2...gxh5, you play 3.fxg7, and again the pawn promotes. If after 1.g6! Black instead plays, 1...fxg6 then 2.h6! means that White promotes the c- or h-pawn. This generally only works if the defending King is too far away to catch the pawn pushing for promotion.

Next another ending involving only King and pawns. (See diagram 306.)

This is a position that I give to most of my

pupils to solve. What is important here is that White has the possibility of creating a distant passed pawn on the Queenside, where he has two pawns against one.

The correct way to secure the win is: **1.a4! Kd6 2.a5 Kxd5 3.a6!!** This is an important finesse.

3...c4 4.b6 Black cannot stop White from promoting one of these pawns. For example, if he tries 4...Kc6, White replies 5.bxa7, and the pawn on a6 prevents Black's King from getting to b7. However, 3.b6? does not work, for Black will play 3...axb6 and after 4.a6 Kc6 he will catch the stray pawn.

'The Square'

Knowing some of the basic rules of endgames is an enormous help in spotting finesses and tricks, and in deciding the right way to go about things. For instance, when considering whether or not you can catch an opponent's passed pawn it is not necessary to count the number of moves to see who will win the race. All you need to know is whether your King is in what's called 'the square'. In the following position Black can easily catch White's passed pawn, whether or not it is White or Black to move. Black is already in the square delineated by a3–f3–f8–a8. (See diagram 307.)

In diagram 308, however, Black can only catch the runaway pawn if it is his turn to move. On this occasion 'the square' is formed by a5–d5–d8–a8 and, if it is White to move, Black is outside it. If it is his turn to play, however, Black simply moves into 'the square' with 1...Kd5.

If the passed pawn is on its starting square, for instance a2, you must allow for the fact that it can move two squares for its first move and you will not be in the square!

Diagram 306

Diagram 307

Diagram 308

Diagram 309

Diagram 310

A Passed Rook Pawn

A King and Rook pawn (either on the a- or h-file), against a lone King is drawn if the defending King is near enough. In the next diagram White has managed to get his King to the queening square, a1, and nothing Black can do will shift it. The position is drawn. (See diagram 309.)

But even in diagram 310, where Black has got in front of the White King it makes no difference. To win this ending Black has to be able to play his own King to b1; and White can prevent that by oscillating between c1 and c2.

Using this knowledge should help you to solve the endgame study shown in diagram 311. Black is threatening to play a1, promoting his pawn to a Queen, but White has a winning position if he can find the correct first move. If you want to solve this puzzle yourself cover the page below the diagram first.

White simply plays, **1.Ra1!** and follows **…Kxa1** with **2.Kc2!** blocking in the black King. Now the game continues:

2…h5 3.Kc1 h4 4.Kc2 h3 5.Kc1
Zugzwang!

5…g5 6.h5 g4 7.h6 g3 8.h7 g2 9.h8=Q#

Diagram 311

A Pawn On The Seventh Rank

Winning with a pawn on the seventh rank, supported by its King, may look simple, but even here there are a few tricks to be aware of. (See diagram 312.)

In the above position White wins easily by first checking the black King with his Queen. Each time the King moves in front of his pawn, to e1, White brings his King one square nearer, until he reaches d3 or e3 and captures the pawn next move.

1.Qd4+ Ke1 2.Ke6 Kf1 3.Qf4+ Kg1 4.Qe3+ Kf1 5.Qf3+ Ke1 6.Kd5 Kd1 7.Qd3+ Ke1 8.Ke4 Kf2 9.Qe3+ Kf1 10.Qf3+ Ke1 11.Kd3 Next move White plays Qxe2+.

Pitfalls

With a c- or f-pawn on the seventh rank, however (see diagram 313), things are not so simple. For example:

1.Qb4+ Ka1 2.Qc3+ Kb1 3.Qb3+ Ka1! 4.Qxc2 Stalemate!

Because of this stalemate possibility the opposing King can never advance up the board to help capture this cheeky pawn.

Similar possibilities also exist in the case of a and h-pawns. In diagram 314 if White tries 1.Qb5+ there follows Ka1! 2.Kc3, and Black is once more stalemated. So, if you look like getting into an ending pawn race, where your opponent will queen first, try to get your own pawn to the seventh rank and pray that it's an a-, c-, f- or h-pawn!

Diagram 312

Diagram 313

Diagram 314

Diagram 315

Diagram 316

Diagram 317

Stalemate and Passed Pawns

Stalemate possibilities abound in the endgame, and it is this trick, or finesse, that can often help you save a lost cause.

In the next position shown in diagram 315, even though Black is a Bishop and pawn up, his Bishop does not control the queening square, a1, and therefore cannot win. White can simply play Kb2–a1–b2 ad infinitum. Try it yourself.

Knowing that a passed pawn on the a- or h-files cannot promote without a piece controlling the queening square helped a master, Oliver Reeh, save the following game, played in the professional Bundesliga in 1997.

Black has just rather carelessly played 1...Kg3? White seized his chance and replied 2.Nf2! Now 2...Kxf2 leads to stalemate. And if Black tries anything else White plays Nxb4, drawing as in the previous example. Black cannot force home the remaining h-pawn. (See diagram 316.)

THE 'FORTRESS'

A fortress is another trick you can use to thwart an opponent who would otherwise win. In the next position White has achieved a simple fortress position, as shown in diagram 317, which works well because Bishops only control squares of one colour.

So, if Black tries Ke3, White responds 2.Ka1 (not 2.Kf1??, or Black plays Kf3 and winkles White out of his fortress). The game might then continue 2...Ke2 3.Kb2, and so on. Black cannot approach any closer because of stalemate.

A fortress is also possible in a Rook against Queen ending. Although a Queen is far more powerful than a Rook, given the right circumstances the Rook can hold her off. In diagram 318 Black has set up a successful fortress position; the Rook, ably protected by the pawns, prevents the white

King from advancing further up the board and aiding his consort. White can make no progress unless Black foolishly moves his Rook from f6.

ROOK AND KING ENDGAMES
The final two diagrams in this section illustrate two famous and important positions in Rook and King endgames.

The Lucena Position
White dare not play 1.Kf7 as Black can reply 1...Rf3+, after which comes 2.Kg6 Rg3+ etc. Somehow White needs to build a bridge. (See diagram 319.)

1.Re4! Rh1 2.Kf7 Rf1+ 3.Kg6 Rg1+ 4.Kf6 Rf1+ 5.Kg5 Rg1+ 6.Rg4! The bridge between the white King and black Rook is built and the pawn promotes.

The Saveedra Position
In diagram 320 White is threatening to promote, c8. Black's only defence is:

1...Rd6+ 2.Kb5 Not 2.Kc7? or Rd2! wins the pawn and draws.

2...Rd5+ 3.Kb4 Rd4+ 4.Kb3 Rd3+ 5.Kc2! Rd5! Now if 6.c8=Q? there follows Rc4 7.Qxc4: stalemate. The following under-promotion is correct:

6. c8=R! Ra4 7.Kb3 Next comes either Rc1# or Kxa4.

1–0

Diagram 318

Diagram 319

Diagram 320

TEST YOUR
CHESS IQ

At the end of the section on check and checkmate, I set you a little problem. I asked you to checkmate the black King in one move (diagram 41 on page 32). The answer is d7#. The black King cannot move to f7 or f8 because it would still be in check, this time from White's Rook on f1. The squares e7 and d8 are already occupied, by a black pawn and Bishop respectively, and the King cannot capture the pawn giving check because it is protected by the white Rook on a7.

CHECK YOUR ABILITY

The remainder of this chapter is devoted to other problems for you to solve. The answers, and an assessment of how well you have done, are given afterwards. I have started with checkmates in one move, which you should find fairly easy. There are also two-move problems dealing with situations where the next player should be in a winning position – at least – in two moves, together with pins, forks, skewers, back-rank weaknesses, destruction and deflection, as well as questions on openings. Some of the problems are easy and some more difficult. Good luck!

CHECKMATE IN ONE MOVE

PROBLEM 1 (1 POINT)

White to move.

PROBLEM 2 (1 POINT)

White to move.

Problem 3 (2 point)

(a) White to move.
(b) Black to move.

PROBLEM 4 (2 POINTS)

Two problems in one again:
(a) White to move.
(b) Black to move.

PROBLEM 5 (1 POINT)

Clue: to solve this you might have to be a bit of a scholar. White to move.

CHECKMATE IN ONE MOVE (...continued)

PROBLEM 6 (1 POINT)

Clue: you'd be a fool not to get this. White to move.

PROBLEM 7 (1POINT)

Clue: the black King cannot move. White to move.

PROBLEM 8 (2 POINTS)

I've given simple hints for some of the earlier problems, but for this one a clue might help. Just remember, a pawn can be promoted to any piece. White to move.

PROBLEM 9 (1POINT)

White to move. Clue: remember Boden's mate.

PROBLEM 10 (2 POINTS)

You might need a clue here too: the Rook on d8 is pinned. White to move.

PROBLEM 11 (1 POINT)

White to move. No clues for this one – easy peasy!

TWO-MOVE PROBLEMS

PROBLEM 12 (2 POINTS)

White to move: the tactical clue is the unprotected black Queen.

PROBLEM 13 (2 POINTS)

White to move: the tactical clue is the black King, Rook and Bishop all lined up on the same diagonal.

PROBLEM 14 (2 POINTS)

Black to move: the tactical clue is the white King trapped on the back rank – a skewer will finish White off.

PROBLEM 15 (2 POINTS)

Black to move: the tactical clue is Black's Rook and Queen both aiming at White's g2 square.

PROBLEM 16 (2 POINTS)

Black to move and achieve a winning position. Tactical clue: the white King and Queen line up on the same rank.

PROBLEM 17 (2 POINTS)

White to move and checkmate in two moves.

PROBLEM 18 (2 POINTS)

White to move and checkmate in two moves.
Tactical clue: remember how to mate with
two Rooks?

PROBLEM 19 (2 POINTS)

White to move and checkmate in two moves.
Tactical clue: Black's King looks nicely
jammed in along the h-file.

PROBLEM 20 (3 POINTS)

White to move and checkmate in two moves.
This is a little more difficult than some of the
problems so far, but a big tactical clue is the
smothered position of the black King.

PROBLEM 21 (2 POINTS)

White to move and win: the tactical clue
is the unguarded Queen on a5.

TWO-MOVE PROBLEMS (...continued)

PROBLEM 22 (2 POINTS)

Black to move and checkmate in two moves. Once again, remember Boden.

PROBLEM 23 (3 POINTS)

Black has just played **Bxb3**, expecting White to reply Nxb3. What White played instead forced his opponent's instant resignation! What did he play?

PIN AND WIN!

PROBLEM 24 (1 POINT)

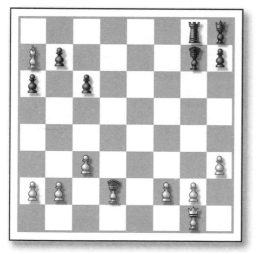

White to move and win in one.

PROBLEM 25 (1 POINT)

White to move and win in one.

PROBLEM 26 (1 POINT)

White to move. Tactical clue: oh dear, just look where Black has placed his Rook.

PROBLEM 27 (1 POINT)

Black has been careless and placed his Queen immediately in front of his King. Teach him a lesson.

PROBLEM 28 (2 POINTS)

Black to move and win in two moves. This problem will need a little more brainpower.

PROBLEM 29 (2 POINTS)

In the position above the white pawn on f2 is already pinned by the black Bishop on b6. Use it to gain a winning advantage.

PIN AND WIN! (...continued)

PROBLEM 30 (5 POINTS)

PROBLEM 31 (1 POINT)

The final problem concerned with pinning is a real tester. What it should do, however, is teach you how valuable a pin can be. The position above comes from a game played in the USSR in 1990, between Miskus (White) and Voronovitch (Black). Miskus won from here in two moves using the power of two pins simultaneously.

The white Bishop pinning the black Knight on f6 should help you win a piece.

EXPLOITING THE FORK

PROBLEM 32 (1 POINT)

One thing Knights cannot do, of course, is pin, but they certainly can fork. One move is all you need.

PROBLEM 33 (1 POINT)

White to move and achieve a large material advantage – a family affair.

PROBLEM 34 (2 POINTS)

A bit more difficult this one; White to move.

PROBLEM 35 (1 POINT)

White to move.

PROBLEM 36 (1 POINT)

Knights do it, Bishops do it, even Rooks and Queens do it (and sometimes pawns and Kings do it). Let's do it. White to move.

EXPLOITING THE FORK (...continued)

PROBLEM 37 (1 POINT)

White wins a pawn.

PROBLEM 38 (1 POINT)

White to move and win Black's Queen.

PROBLEM 39 (1 POINT)

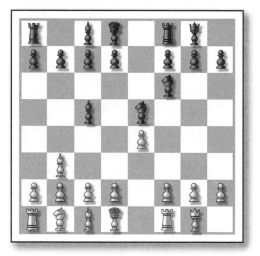

White to move and win a piece.

USE THE SKEWER

PROBLEM 40 (1 point)

White wins a Rook.

PROBLEM 41 (1 POINT)

White wins a Rook.

PROBLEM 42 (2 POINTS)

White is about to promote the pawn on g7, but Black has pinned it with his Queen. Use a skewer to force your pawn home and win.

PROBLEM 43 (3 POINTS)

Black to move and force checkmate or win White's Queen. It's the use of the skewer that makes the difference.

BACK-RANK WEAKNESSES

PROBLEM 44 (2 POINTS)

White, who dominates the d-file, can force victory with his next move.

PROBLEM 45 (2 POINTS)

White forces mate in three moves at most.

PROBLEM 46 (3 POINTS)

White mates in four moves or wins Black's Queen.

PROBLEM 47 (2 POINTS)

The following position came towards the end of a wonderful combination by the great Alekhine. As White I've left you with just the remaining two moves to finish Black off.

DESTRUCTION AND DEFLECTION

PROBLEM 48 (3 POINTS)

Black, to move and win, would just love to get his Rook to h1, but needs a little demolition work first.

PROBLEM 49 (2 POINTS)

You've seen this position earlier, assuming you've been reading this book properly. Black to move and win.

PROBLEM 50 (1 POINT)

White to move and win – an easy-to-see deflection.

PROBLEM 51 (2 POINTS)

White to move and checkmate in two or win Black's Queen.

DESTRUCTION AND DEFLECTION (...continued)

PROBLEM 52 (2 POINTS)

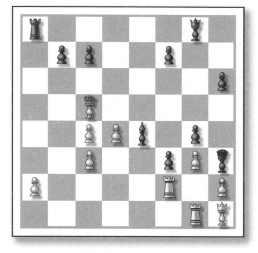

Black to move and win. White is very weak on the white squares near his King. Somehow Black has to 'persuade' one of the defenders to move.

PROBLEM 53 (3 POINTS)

White to move and checkmate in three or win Black's Queen. Two deflections needed.

PROBLEM 54 (2 POINTS)

White to move and checkmate in two; the right move deflects either of two Black defenders, allowing White to apply the *coup de grâce*.

PROBLEM 55 (3 POINTS)

White to move and win: first a destruction then a deflection.

STALEMATES

PROBLEM 56 (2 POINTS)

In the following game White, in a winning position, has rather carelessly just played d6? How can Black now save himself?

PROBLEM 57 (2 POINTS)

White looks like he's moving in for the kill, but Black can save himself. How?

PROBLEM 58 (3 POINTS)

White is about to play b8 and gain another Queen. How does Black cleverly save his bacon?

PROBLEM 59 (1 POINT)

An easy, but effective, stalemate to finish. Black to move.

ENDGAME TEASERS

PROBLEM 60 (1 POINT)

Black to move and win.

PROBLEM 61 (2 POINTS)

Black to move and win the pawn race.

PROBLEM 62 (2 POINTS)

Rook and pawn endings are notoriously difficult to win, especially with a Rook pawn. Black's last move was **Kf7**, a fatal error. What did White play now to ensure victory?

PROBLEM 63 (5 POINTS)

Finding the right move in this position helped White to gain the Grandmaster title. What was the move that saved White from losing this game?

OPENINGS

OPENING 1 (2 POINTS)

The position below has been reached via the following moves: **1.e4 e5 2.Nf3 Nc6 3.Bc4 Bc5 4.c3** What is the opening?

OPENING 2 (2 POINTS)

The following moves were the start of a game between Pillsbury and Wolf: **1.d4 d5 2.c4 e6 3.Nc3 Nf6 4.Bg5 Nbd7 5.Nf3 Be7** What is the opening?

OPENING 3 (2 POINTS)

This is a trappy opening, but what is it? The position was arrived at via the following moves: **1.e4 e6 2.d4 d5 3.e5 c5 4.c3 Nc6 5.Nf3 Qb6 6.Bd3**

OPENING 4 (2 POINTS)

This opening is named for two different players and the position is reached after the following: **1.d4 d5 2.Nf3 Nf6 3.e3 e6 4.Bd3 c5 5.b3** Name the opening.

Answers to problems

Problems Nos.	Answers/Points
1	1.Qxg7# (1 point)
2	1.Qxh7# (1 point)
3a	1.Rh8# (1 point)
3b	1...Qa2# (1 point)
4a	1.Qg7# (1 point)
4b	1...Qh2# (1 point)
5	1.Qxf7# (Scholar's mate) (1 point)
6	1.Qh5# (Fool's mate pattern) (1 point)
7	1.Ng6# (the pawn on h7 is pinned) (1 point)
8	1.c8=N# (2 points)
9	1.Bh6# (1 point)
10	1.Qxd7# (2 points)
11	1.Nf7# (1 point)
12	1.Rh8+ Kxh8 2.Ng6+ Kg8 3.Qxc7 (2 points)
13	1.Rxe7 Kxe7 2.Bxc5+ wins the Rook on b4 (2 points)
14	1...Ra1+ 2.Qxa1 Rh1+ wins White's Queen (2 points)
15	1...Qg2+ 2.Kxg2 Bxe5+ 3.Kh1 Bxd6 (not 1...Be5+? 2.Qxe5+) wins for White (2 points)
16	1...Rg2+ 2.Kxg2 Ne3+ wins White's Queen (2 points)
17	1.Qg8+! Rxg8 2.Nf7# (2 points)
18	1.Qxh7+ Kxh7 2.Rh1# (2 points)
19	1.Qxh7+ Kxh7 2.hxg5# (2 points)
20	1.Rh6 gxh6 2.Rxh7# (3 points)
21	1.Qh5+ Kf8 2.Nd7+ Ke7 3.Qxa5

Problems Nos.	Answers/Points
	or Kg7 2.Ne6+ Bxe6 3.Qxa5 or 1...Rg6 2.Rg1 wins the Rook (2 points)
22	1...Qc3+ 2.bxc3 Ba3# (2 points)
23	1.e7+! Kxe7 2.Nc6+ wins the exchange (2 points)
24	1.Bd4 (1 point)
25	1.Bb5 (1 point)
26	1.Bc4 (1 point)
27	1.Rfe1 (or Rae1) (1 point)
28	1.Bg5 f4 2.Bxf4 Qxf4 3.Qxb2# (2 points)
29	1.Qxg3+ Kh1 30.Bf3+ (2 points)
30	1.Qh6!! Qxf6 2.Nh5 (If 2...Nxh5 3.Qxf8#; if 2...gxh5 3.Qxh7#; and if 2...Qe7 3.Qg7# (5 points)
31	1.e5 (1 point)
32	1.Ne4+ (1 point)
33	1.Ne6+ (1 point)
34	1.Nd6!! (If 1...Bxd6 2.Qg7#, and if 1...Rxd6 2.Qxc8 wins the exchange) (2 points)
35	1.Nxf7 (1 point)
36	1.Qd4+ (1 point)
37	1.Bc5+ (1 point)
38	1.Bxd6+ (1 point)
39	1.d4 (1 point)
40	1.Be3 (or Ra6+) (1 point)
41	1.Re7+ (1 point)
42	1.Qg1+! Qxg1 2.g8=Q+ (2 points)
43	1...g4+! 2.Kxg4 Bh5+ 3.Kxh5 Qg5# (3 points)
44	1.Qa7! R(or Q)xa7 2.Rxd8+ and 3.Rxd8# (or 1...Qc8

Problems Nos.	Answers/Points
	2.QxR QxQ 3.Rxd8 Qxd8 4.Rxd8# (2 points)
45	1.Qxf7+ Rxf7 2.Rd8+ Rf8 3.Rxf8# (2 points)
46	1.Qxd5+! Qxd5 2.Ne7+ Kh8 3.Rf8+ Qg8 4.Rxg8# (3 points)
47	1...Rxf8+ 2. Kxf8 Qd8# (2 points)
48	1.Qxf4 gxf4 2.Rh5 and mate on h1 cannot be avoided (3 points)
49	1...Nd4! 2.Nxd4 Qh2# (If 2.Qd1 Nxf3+ 3.Qxf3 Qh2#) (2 points)
50	1.Re8+ Rxe8 2.Qxd5 (1 point)
51	1.Qxf8+ Qxf8 2.Rxh7# (2 points)
52	1...Rxa2 2.Rxa2 f2+ 3.Rg2 Qxg2# 2
53	1.Nd7+ Bxd7 2.Qxc8+ Bxc8 3.Re8# (3 points)
54	1.Re8+ Bxe8 2.Qf8# or 1.Re8+ Qxe8 2.Qxf6# (2 points)
55	1.Rxe7 Qxe7 2.Bxc5 Qxc5 3. Qf6+ Kg8 4.Qg7# (3 points)
56	1.Bc6+ Qxc6 2.Rg1+ (2 points)
57	1...Rd1+ 2.Kxd1 or 1.Kc2 Rd2+ and Black can check forever (2 points)
58	1...g3+ 2.Qxg3 Qg1+ 3.Kxg1 (3 points)
59	1...Nc6+ 2.bxc6 (2 points)
60	1...Kc3 2.Kd1 Kb2 (covering the queening square) and now Black plays c3–c2–c1=Q (1 point)

Problems Nos.	Answers/Points
61	1...g4! 2.hxg4 h3 and White cannot prevent Black promoting on h1 (2 points)
62	1.Rh8! Rxa7 2.Rh7+ Ke6 3.Rxa7 or 1...Kg7 2.a8=Q (2 points)
63	1.Rh4! Rxb4+ 2.Kc5 Rxh4 stalemate (5 points)

Opening 1	Giucco Piano (see page 60) (2 points)
Opening 2	Queen's Gambit Declined (see pages 76–77) (2 points)
Opening 3	French Defence (see page 88) (2 points)
Opening 4	Colle-Zukertort (see pages 74–75) (2 points)

ASSESSMENT

Points scored	Comment
115–120	A Grandmaster in the making (or you've been cheating!)
100–114	Master potential
90–99	A possible county player
75–89	Club player potential
60–74	At least you've read the book
45–59	Still plenty to enjoy
Below 45	You're just not trying! Read the book again.

Don't take the assessment too seriously – it's only intended as a rough guide to your potential.

THE WAY
FORWARD

If you get hooked on chess, as millions of people around the world have done, you will want to maximize your talent through practice. Each of the following can help you do so.

CHESS CLUBS

Don't make the mistake of waiting until you are good enough to join a club; rather, join a club to become good enough! You will find clubs in most towns and cities around the world but, like everything else, they vary. Look for a friendly club; one that attracts lots of youngsters is always a good sign.

CHESS COACHES

Your next step should be to find a reputable coach. Remember, however, that a good player, a Grandmaster or International Master, does not necessarily equate to being a good coach – teaching is one skill, playing is another. Before you commit yourself to any coach try to discover how many pupils of theirs have turned out to be good players.

The cost of coaching depends on where you live and whether the coach is a titled player (an International Master or Grandmaster).

CHESS PROBLEMS

So you've joined a friendly club and found a competent coach. What's next? Well, as International Master, Mike Basman says, 'chess is a game played in the head'. To play well it's vital to be able to recognize, even if only subconsciously, the numerous patterns that appear on the chessboard. The best way to learn these is to attempt problems regularly. (My own pupils regularly receive problems as part of their 'homework'.) There are lots of books of chess problems, each aimed at different playing strengths. To start with, buy something basic, one with simple mate-in-one and mate-in-two problems. If you can get hold of a copy, Judit Polgar's *Chess Training in 5,333 + 1 positions* is excellent value, if rather large and heavy.

NATIONAL ASSOCIATIONS

The next step is to join your national chess association or federation. The national body responsible for chess in any country should be able to keep you in touch with tournaments and chess clubs useful to you. The Federation Internationale des Echecs (FIDE) is the international chess association, the British Chess Federation (BCF) is responsible for English chess and the United States Chess Federation (USCF) for chess in the United States. Website of other federations are given in the section on Internet chess (see pages 177–179).

NEWSPAPERS AND MAGAZINES

Another worthwhile step is to invest in a newspaper that carries a regular chess column and subscribe to a chess magazine. Both of these should help you to learn what is going on in the world of chess and, by playing through the games you come across, you will acquire a wealth of knowledge that will prove invaluable to you later on.

COMPETITIONS

Finally, whenever you can, enter novice competitions.

Practical tips

Each of the above should help you to improve as a player and gain even further enjoyment from this magical game. This sections offers more specific advice, which you might like to photocopy and, initially at least, take with you to matches, memorizing what you can before you start.

TIP 1
Every time, after your opponent has moved always ask yourself, why has he/she done that? Always ask yourself, what is the threat? Do not move until you know the answers to these questions.

TIP 2
Do not play the first move that comes into your head; check out some other moves first.

TIP 3
Examine every corner of the board, not just the area where you think the action is.

TIP 4
Don't move for the sake of it – try to have a real plan relevant to the strengths and weaknesses of the position.

TIP 5
When your opponent plays a move in the opening that you have never seen before, don't panic; they may not know the opening either!

TIP 6
Knowing the main ideas behind openings is usually more important than knowing every move by heart – even Grandmasters do not know everything.

TIP 7
After every game, as soon as possible, go through it by yourself and correct any errors on your score sheet. That way your coach will be able to make some sense of things and give you some positive help.

TIP 8
As soon as possible, go through your games and try to find out what better moves you might have played.

TIP 9
Try to play through at least one game per day, from a newspaper or magazine – you'll be surprised at what you learn.

TIP 10
Regularly attempt problems – this will help develop your combinational skills.

TIP 11
Remember that losing is not a crime; every loss is a signpost to victory.

COMPUTER CHESS

THE FIRST CHESS COMPUTERS

It was sometime in the late 1960s, I believe, that the famous British journalist Bernard Levin wrote a piece about the possibilities of a computer playing chess well enough to compete successfully against a human master. Levin was highly scornful about the possibility, pointing to the immense complexity of the game of chess and truly enormous number of possible moves at the chessboard.

The article was sparked by interest generated when the Grandmaster, Mikhail Botvinnik – an ex-World Champion and qualified electrical engineer – began exploring the possibility of producing a high-quality chess-playing machine. Part of the aim behind this was to discover how the human mind worked – a goal that has still not been achieved!

A few years after Levin's article the International Master David Levy wagered £1,000 that no computer could be produced within the next ten years able to beat him at chess; a bold claim indeed.

Since then, things have moved on, and today the best chess-playing computers have their own tournaments and Elo ratings, equivalent to some of the best Grandmasters!

Strengths and weaknesses of computers

In essence a computer is simply a superb calculating machine, but in terms of playing chess it does have flaws. In positions involving tactics it can 'out-think' the human almost every time. But computers are not so good in deep strategic positions involving the generation of ideas. They have no imagination so cannot think creatively or come up with new ideas in the opening. Grandmasters now use this knowledge to good effect in human versus computer matches.

The current World Champion, Vladimir Kramnik, played an unusual move in the opening of one of his games against the computer, Deep Fritz, and soon had it floundering. Its opening database just wasn't up to it. In an advanced chess match – an idea dreamed up by Garry Kasparov, where each player uses a computer to help him in his game – Vishy Anand defeated the Spanish GM, Alexei Shirov, by ignoring his computer's advice! This was a difficult endgame, which required calculation of many different lines up to 14 moves deep. The computer simply couldn't cope with the problem. Anand used his experience and intuition, things a computer doesn't possess.

In diagram 321 Anand now played **33.Nxg5!!** after which the game continued **hxg5 34.Bxg5 Nxb3 35.h4 Na1 36.Bc1 Nb3 37.Be3 Na5 38.g5 Nc4 39.Bc1** and Shirov resigned. (If 39...Kd7, there follows 40.h5 Ke8 41.h6 Bxh6 42.gxh6 Kf8 43.h7, and White promotes.) The computer was

BUYING A COMPUTER OF CHESS PROGRAMME

- Chess-playing computers come in a wide range of types and prices, from small hand-held computers to touch-sensory boards with built-in computers.

- Or you can buy PC programmes like Fritz, Chessbase, and a host of others. All of these computer 'players' have an approximate Elo or national rating to give you some idea of the programme/version that might suit you, and the more expensive ones come with a range of settings, including training levels, coaching functions etc.

- Though not the same as playing against another human, computers can give you the opportunity to practise and, perhaps, improve your chess. If you wish to invest in a computer you would do well to contact a specialist chess outlet rather than buy one from a normal high street retailer.

---

incapable of dealing with all the possibilities in the original position.

Grandmasters have learned to avoid tactical positions (short-term plans involving combinations and so forth, which the computer is able to calculate easily) as much as possible and often outplay computers by keeping the game along strategic (long-term positional) lines. In difficult positions a human player may well try out some double-edged and possibly risky manoeuvre, in an attempt to unsettle and confuse his or her opponent. Computers are incapable of such originality and just struggle on, getting into an ever-deeper mess.

Of course computers have other advantages apart from their superior calculating speed: they don't get tired or ill and are unaffected by personal problems, simply playing the position in front of them. They have been a big help in developing chess to new heights, helping players to learn with the aid of software and analysing games played to improve a player's knowledge and skill.

Diagram 321

Chess computers in action

To close this section, here's a game between the World Champion, Vladimir Kramnik, and the computer, Deep Fritz. The opening is Queen's Gambit Accepted.

Vladimir Kramnik–Deep Fritz
6 October 2002

1.d4 d5 2.c4 dxc4 3.Nf3 Nf6 4.e3 e6 5.Bxc4 c5 6.0–0 a6 7.dxc5!? This is a move that Kramnik had played with success against Kasparov.

7...Qxd 18.Rxd1 Bxc5 9.Kf1! This is an utterly brilliant conception; it takes the computer out of its 'book'.

9...b5 10.Be2 Bb7 11.Nbd2 Nbd7 12.Nb3 I am not an expert in the Queen's Gambit Accepted but, according to International Master Malcolm Pein, writing in *Chess Monthly*, this move is a 'bit unusual'. Fritz clearly wasn't expecting it and replied with an absurd move...

12...Bf8?? ...believing that Kramnik would now have to return his Knight to d2, after which it would be possible for Fritz to repeat moves and gain an early draw. Instead of Bf8 any reasonably strong human chess player would have played 12...Be7.

13.a4! Black's last move means that it will be some time before the Rook on h8 sees any action. Kramnik immediately attacks the weakened Queenside pawns.

13...b4 Capturing the pawn on a4 will leave Black's a pawn very weak indeed.

14.Nfd2 Heading for c4.

14...Bd5 15.f3 Bd6 16.g3 e5 17.e4 Be6 18.Nc4 Bc7 19.Be3 a5 20.Nc5 Nxc5 21.Bxc5 Nd7 22.Nd6+ Kf8 23.Be3 Bxd6 24.Rxd6 Ke7 25.Rad1 Rhc8 26.Bb5 Nc5 27.Bc6 Bc4+ 28.Ke1 Nd3+ 29.R1xd3 Bxd3 30.Bc5 Bc4 31.Rd4+ Kramnik forces a Rook and pawn endgame.

31...Kf6 32.Rxc4 Rxc6 33.Be7+ Kxe7 34.Rxc6 Kd7 35.Rc5 f6 36.Kd2 White has a big advantage in this Rook and pawn endgame (see diagram 322). His Rook is far more active than Black's and, sooner or later, White's King will take up a dominant position on c4, allowing his Rook to penetrate behind enemy lines and win at least one of Black's pawns. Any strong human player in such a passive position as Black finds himself in would sacrifice a pawn to activate his or her pieces and set his or her opponent practical problems, but computers cannot help being 'materialistic' and its this weakness that leads to Fritz's downfall.

From the above position Kramnik used his expert technical endgame skill to win a pawn and the game. Deep Fritz resigned in the following position.

Kramnik's last move (see diagram 323) was **57.Rd5+**. This forces the exchange of Rooks and Fritz could easily calculate that White would be left with an easy technical win. A possible finish might be:

Diagram 322

Diagram 323

57...Rxd5 58.exd5 Kd6 59.b4 axb4+ 60.Kxb4 Kxd5 61.Kb5 f5

62.a5 e4 63.a6 and White will reach a8 and promote his pawn to a Queen, giving check to Black's King and preventing Fritz making any further progress with its own pawn.

CHESS ON THE INTERNET

If the World Wide Web and the Internet hadn't been invented it's almost a certainty that some chess-playing computer programmer would have come up with the idea sooner or later – the Internet could well have been made for chess.

In modern times most important matches and tournaments can be followed live on the Internet, with the larger tournaments updated daily. You can also log on to various sites for information on books, software and chess equipment generally. But the real plus for the average chess player, to my mind, is the fact that you can play chess on the Internet at any time of night or day, against a wide range of playing strengths; even, occasionally, an International Master or Grandmaster!

There is a wide variety of chess-related sites on the Internet, catering for all ages, levels of expertise and requirements so I have divided them into groups

SUPPLIERS, PUBLISHERS AND CLUBS

Not surprisingly most of the specialist chess suppliers, publishers and chess magazines also have their own sites. Perhaps more surprising is the fact that quite a few clubs have their own sites too. The most famous of these is probably the Manhattan Chess Club, which can be found at www.manhattanchessclub.com.

COACHING AND TRAINING SITES

For those of you coming to chess for the first time the most useful sites may well be the coaching and training sites. There are quite a few of these across the world and two stand out.

The first is ChessKids Academy at www.chesskids.com – an excellent site for under 12s, although any beginner could also benefit from visiting ChessKids Academy.

The second site of interest is Chess Doctor, which can be found at www.chessdoctor.com. This site has five main sections:

1 Chess Downloads, where you can view for free up to 50 games that have previously been analysed
2 Chess Secrets
3 Chess Instruction
4 Chess Analysis
5 Chess Lessons, in this last section, Chess Doctor offers coaching at $20 per hour

CORRESPONDENCE CHESS SITES

If you want to try your hand at correspondence chess you can log on to www.correspondencechess.com but this is just one of many websites (see your national organization).

MISCELLANEOUS SITES

There are numerous other sites of interest for chess players, including sites for the following: chess openings, famous players, general chess interest, chess problems and problem composers, chess software and playing chess on the Internet.

Grandmasters online!

I mentioned earlier that one of the joys of playing online was the possibility of playing against a Grandmaster. In 1999, the public played against then world champion, Garry Kasparov in the much-publicized Kasparov–The World match. The World consisted of members of the public joining the Microsoft Network to vote on moves suggested by a team of top juniors, which included Etienne Bacrot, Florin Felecan, Irina Krush and Elisabeth Pahtz. Etienne Bacrot is now a Grandmaster ranked 33 in the world, while Irina Krush is an International Master and Grandmaster, who was recently 13th in the women's world rankings.

GARRY KASPAROV–THE WORLD
(Played online on Internet Microsoft Network, 1999)

1.e4 c5 2.Nf3 d6 3.Bb5+ This is the Moscow Attack variation of the Sicilian Defence.

3...Bd7 4.Bxd7+ Qxd7 5.c4 White's objective here is to take total control of the square, d5.

5...Nc6 6.Nc3 Nf6 7.0–0 g6 8.d4 cxd4 The game has now transposed into the Dragon variation of the Sicilian Defence; White's set-up is called the Maroczy Bind.

9.Nxd4 Bg7 10.Nde2 Qe6 11.Nd5 Qxe4 12.Nc7+ Kd7 13.Nxa8 Qxc4 Black has destroyed White's bind in the centre, gaining two pawns and a Knight for one Rook. The material balance, in terms of points, is equal, but after White's next move Black will have to contend with a weakened Queenside.

ONLINE CHESS

The best-known site for playing online is the Internet Chess Club, which can be found at www.chessclub.com. This is a commercial site but it offers a free trial for one week. When I last looked there were 1,027 players playing online, including six Grandmasters and twenty-three International Masters! However, if this is too heady a mix for you, you can always try www.freechess.org.

14.Nb6+ axb6 15.Nc3 Ra8 16.a4 Ne4 17.Nxe4 Qxe4 18.Qb3 f5 19.Bg5 Qb4 20.Qf7 Be5 21.h3 Rxa4 22.Rxa4 Qxa4 23.Qxh7 Bxb2 24.Qxg6 Qe4 25.Qf7 Bd4 26.Qb3 f4 27.Qf7 Be5 28.h4 b5 The race begins!

29.h5 Qc4 30.Qf5+ Qe6 31.Qxe6 Kxe6 32.g3 fxg3 33.fxg3 b4 34.Bf4 Bd4+ 35.Kh1 b3 36.g4 Kd5 37.g5 e6 38.h6 Ne7 39.Rd1 e5 40.Be3 Kc4 41.Bxd4 exd4 42.Kg2 b2 43.Kf3 Kc3 44.h7 Ng6 45.Ke4 Kc2 46.Rh1 d3 47.Kf5 b1(Q) 48.Rxb1 Kxb1 49.Kxg6 d2 50.h8(Q) d1(Q) 51.Qh7 b5 52.Kf6+ Kb2 53.Qh2+ Ka1 54.Qf4 b4 55.Qxb4 Qf3+ 56.Kg7 d5 57.Qd4+ Kb1 58.g6 Qe4 59.Qg1+ Kb2 60.Qf2+ Kc1 61.Kf6 d4 62.g7 Black resigns.

1–0

A remarkable and historic online game.

CORRESPONDENCE CHESS

AN OVERVIEW

Correspondence or postal chess, although probably not so popular as it once was, before computers and the Internet came along, still has a substantial following.

It may seem odd to send your moves by mail to someone you will probably never meet and is, of course, very slow compared to over-the-board chess. However, serious correspondence players often have 20 or 30 games on the go at once, so there is a card or letter, containing a move from one of their many opponents, landing on the door mat most days.

Correspondence chess has its own International Master and Grandmaster ratings and, at its highest level, can produce games of superb quality.

ADVANTAGES OF CORRESPONDENCE CHESS

Even with plenty of time to study each move, correspondence games, like the one above, are often still full of errors and can be over quite quickly. In other words, correspondence chess does not have to be long-winded and tedious. Furthermore, it has plenty of points in its favour, just some of which are listed below and overleaf.

- It is an excellent playing medium for those who are housebound or incapacitated.
- It is also ideal for those players – some really gifted – who don't achieve their best due to nerves taking over in tense over-the-board situations. These sort of pressures don't exist in correspondence chess and the possibility of ruining a good game because of time-trouble panic is reduced to nil.
- You can work on your postal games at times that suit you.

• You don't have to memorize huge amounts of opening theory. It is quite legitimate to refer to books and databases to help you, and this therefore affords you a perfect opportunity to experiment in the opening.

• Postal chess gives you every opportunity to analyse positions in depth – excellent training for over-the-board chess.

The only thing that spoils modern day postal chess, in my view, is the unsporting use of computers by some players to help them analyse tricky tactical positions. Somehow this practice needs to be stopped.

Postal chess has its own leagues, tournaments and county matches and its own national organizations. If this form of chess appeals to you, you can find your national correspondence association through your national chess body.

Examples of correspondence chess

To finish this section I give two examples of correspondence games. The first – full of tactical clues – was played in the 1928–29 season, and is one of my favourites. The second is a postal game of my own, published in *Chess* magazine in 1961.

Example 1

NN–MULLER, H.
English Opening

1.c4 e5 2.Nf3 Nc6 3.Nc3 Nf6 4.d4 cxd4 5.Nxd4 Bb4 6.Nxc6 bxc6 7.g3? Many errors occur in the first ten moves, but inexperienced players rarely spot them, because they are in a hurry to reach the middlegame. In diagram 324 Black realizes that White's last move is an error, because placing his Bishop on g2 will seriously weaken his e2 square.

Diagram 324

7...Qe7! 8.Bg2 Ba6 9.Qd3 d5 10.b3
Diagram 325 shows the result of White's serious error on move 7: the pawn on c4 is pinned by Black's Bishop on a6, the Knight on c3 is pinned by Black's Bishop on b4, and the a6 Bishop combines with the Queen to put pressure on White's e2 square.

10...d4!! Adding more pressure to the Knight on c3.

11.Qxd4 If 11.Bxc6+, then Kf8 12.Bxa8 Bxc3+ 13. Kf1 Bxa1, and Black is a piece to the good.

11...Rd8 12.Bxc6+ Kf8 13.Bd5 Rxd5 If 14.cxd5, then Qxe2#, and if 14.Qe3 there follows Qxe3 15.fxe3 Bxc3+ and 16...Bxa1. White resigns

0–1

Example 2

HEMMINGSEN, A (Glostrup CC, Denmark)**–LEVENS, DAVID** (Cedars CC, England)

1.d4 Nf6 2.c4 e6 3.Nc3 Bb4 The Nimzo-Indian Defence.

4.e3 0–0 5.Bd2? This move is quite unnecessary in this variation.

5...d5 6.Nf3 Nc6 7.Bd3 dxc4 8.Bxc4 Qe7 9.Qc2 e5! A pawn break that challenges White's centre.

10.d5 Na5!? 11.Bd3 c6 12.a3 Bd6 13.b4 cxd5 14.e4 d4 15.Nd5 Nxd5 16.exd5 White's 15th move has freed

Black's central pawns for the assault which now follows.

16...e4! If now 17.Bxe4, then f5.

17.0–0? Almost certainly the losing move.

17...exf3 18.Bxh7+ The Knight on a5 remains taboo throughout the game; if 18.bxa5 then Bxh2+ 19.Kxh2 Qh4+ 20.Kg1 fxg2 21.Kxg2 Ba3+ 22.Kg1 Qg4+, and mate next move.

18...Kh8 19.Be4 Qh4 20.g3 Qh5 21.Qd3 Bg4 22.h3 f5! White's white squares around his King are so weak it's important to maintain the pawn on f3.

23.hxg4 fxg4 24.Rfb1 Bxg3 This had to be played before...Qh3 so that Black's Queen could capture on g3.

25.fxg3 Qh3 26.Kf2 Qg2+ 27.Ke1 f2+ 28.Kd1 f1=Q+ 29.Qxf1 Rxf1+ White resigns.

0–1

Diagram 325

CHESS VARIANTS – SOME DIFFERENT FUN WAYS OF PLAYING CHESS

Although it's a long time since I played anything other than normal chess – apart that is from Lightning Chess, Blitz Chess and Rapidplay, which all follow the normal basic rules of chess – many of the youngsters I coach and come across at different events are often found playing one chess variant or another.

LOSING (SUICIDE) CHESS

This is very popular among the youngsters I meet. As its name implies, the aim of this variation is to lose all of your men before your opponent does. According to David Pritchard's excellent book *Popular Chess Variants*, there are just four rules:

- Capturing is compulsory, though players may choose between alternatives.
- Check is abolished; the King behaves like any other piece.
- A pawn can promote to a King!
- The object is to lose all your men or be without a legal move – thus being in stalemate would win.

SWAP CHESS

This is a variant of chess that is played in pairs and can be great fun. To play it you need two sets and four players divided into two teams of two; one player of each team has the white pieces, while their partners have the black pieces. When a piece is taken that piece is handed to the other's partner to be placed on their board, when and where he or she seems fit! The only proviso is that the introduced piece may not be placed on any square within the opponent's first two ranks. Otherwise the rules are the same as normal chess. If one partner wins and the other loses then the match is declared a draw.

PROGRESSIVE CHESS

Progressive Chess, or Scotch Chess as I've heard it called, is a variation that I believe

---

An example of losing (suicide) chess

This variation turns chess on its head, but may teach beginners what to avoid doing...

In this endgame position (see diagram 326) it is Black to move. No matter where he now puts his remaining Bishop he is lost.

1...Ba7 2.b6 Bxb6 3.c5 Bxc5 4.d4 Bxd4 5.e3 Bxe3 6.Kf2 Bxf2

1–0

Diagram 326

An example of progressive chess

The following is a seven-move game played under the Italian rules.

White: **1.d4**
Black: **2.Nc6, Nf6**
White: **3.Bg5, e4, Nf3**
Black: **4.d5, dxe4, Qxd4, Qxd1+**
White: **5.Kxd1, Bxf6, Bxg7, Bxh8, Ng5**
Black: **6.f6, fxg5, e5, Ke7, Be6, Rd8+**
White: **7.Kc1, b3, Kb2, Ka3, Nd2, Nc4, Bf6#**

Diagram 327

White's crafty move shown in diagram 327 was placing his King on a3, in line with Black's Bishop on f8. Now, wherever Black plays his King he will put White in check on his first move (illegal in this Italian variation); therefore, he is checkmated.

has some practical value for real chess. Indeed, I have introduced it into some of my group coaching sessions as a way of helping players to develop the ability to think ahead. The rules are as follows.

- White starts with one move.
- Black then makes two consecutive moves, either with the same man or two different ones.
- White now makes three moves and so on. Thus White always makes an odd number of moves and Black an even number.
- A player's turn ends immediately he gives check regardless of the number of moves made. The Italian version of the game, which I believe requires more skill, states, 'a player may not check before the last

move of a sequence'. What this means in practical terms is that if a player is in check at the start of his turn, and the only move available is one that gives check, then it is checkmate.

Games of Progressive Chess should not last longer than 10 or 11 moves, if you are planning ahead properly. For example:

White: **1.e4**
Black: **2.e5, Nf6??**
White: **3.Bc4, Qh5, Qf7#**

If White opens 1.e4 a sensible reply would be 2.d5, Nc6.

KRIEGSPIEL

This needs two players, an umpire and three sets and boards. All three sets are set up alongside each other with the white pieces on the same side on all three boards. The two outside sets are screened from each other and the umpire stands on White's side of the middle board from where he can observe both of the other two sets. Neither of the two players can see what the other has moved and herein lies the fun; especially for spectators.

After each player has made an opening move, White may ask the umpire, 'Any?' meaning are there any pawn captures? The umpire plays all the moves on his board unseen by the players and so at any given time he is the only one of the three who knows the true position of the game. So if the game has started 1.e4 d5 the umpire, in reply to White's 'any?' would now reply, 'You may try.' Had Black's first move been 1...c5 say the umpire would simply reply no. However because the umpire has replied, 'you may try' White must attempt at least one capture and may go on trying until a capture is effected. If, in the instance given,

White first tries, 2.exf5 and gets a 'no' from the umpire he now knows that Black has opened 1...d5 and would be wise to play this move on his own board. If, instead, White had tried 2.exd5 the umpire would announce, 'White has played and captured on d5.' This is the only information that an umpire is allowed to give, but at no time must he say what has been captured or what man made the capture; only en passant captures must be announced.

A player may try a capture without asking the umpire, 'Any?' Checks are announced by the umpire according to the direction(s) of the attack only: for example, according to the situation, he might say 'You are in check along the rank/file/long diagonal/short diagonal/by a Knight.' Note here that the umpire does not reveal the square of the attacking piece.

Bluff plays a large part in Kriegspiel but should a player ask, 'Any?' when a pawn capture is impossible the umpire may say, 'Nonsense' or 'Impossible.'

Though it may seem largely a game of chance, in the hands of experienced players Kriegspiel requires a good deal of skill.

GLOSSARY

Advantage A feature of the position that is likely to encourage a player to continue to strive for victory.

Analysis The result of working out several possible variations of a given position.

Algebraic notation The modern form of recording a game of chess.

Annotation Comments and analysis on a given position after particular moves in a game.

Back-rank mate A checkmate on the final rank of the board when the King is hemmed in by its own pawns. (See pages 40–41.)

Backward pawn A pawn, which, though not isolated, is behind any of its own pawns on adjacent files.

Bad bishop A Bishop that is hemmed in by its own pawns, which are on the same colour as the 'bad Bishop'.

Bind A situation or formation that prevents the other side making any active plan.

Bishop pair Two Bishops working together on the same side; very powerful on an open board.

Blockade To place a piece in front of a pawn, especially a passed pawn, to prevent its further advance.

Blocked position A position in which many pawns of each side are locked together, preventing ease of movement by the black and white pieces.

Blunder A very poor move that throws away an advantage or loses the game.

Breakthrough A means of making progress against a tough defence; often initiated by a sacrifice of a piece or pawn.

Brilliancy A spectacular game of chess (see 'The Evergreen' game in the chapter on the middlegame – see pages 116–117). A brilliancy may contain plenty of small mistakes.

Castling A special move in chess involving a King and Rook of the same colour. (See pages 16–17.)

Centralization The placing of pieces in the centre of the board.

Centre The squares e4, d4, e5 and d5.

Checkmate The ultimate aim of a game of chess; a position where one King is in check and cannot escape from check by any means.

Classical A school of thought that believes that occupation of the centre is vital.

Clearance A means of exchanging or sacrificing to clear lines for other pieces to invade.

Closed games Openings beginning with 1.d4 but excluding the Indian Defences.

Closed positions See 'Blocked position', above.

Combination A forcing sequence of moves usually involving various tactical motifs.
Compensation Strategic or tactical benefits usually gained from some sacrifice.

Connected pawns Pawns that can support each other on adjacent files.

Correspondence chess A form of chess that is carried on by post (usually using postcards), fax or email; it is an excellent way to enjoy chess for anyone who is housebound, but also enjoyed by thousands of others.

Counter gambit A gambit by Black.

Counterplay Potential drawing or winning chances for a player under pressure from his or her opponent.

Defence Moves played in response to threats posed by one's opponent.

Development A means of bringing your army into battle – usually the quicker the better.

Diagonal opposition A situation in an endgame where the opposing Kings are separated by an odd number of squares along a diagonal. The player with the opposition is the one not to move.

Discovered attack A move when one member of your army steps out of the way of another member, allowing both of them to attack two other members of the opposition army at the same time. (See page 40.)

Discovered check The same as a discovered attack except that the attack is now on the opposing King.

Distant opposition An endgame situation where the opposing Kings are standing on the same file or rank with three or five squares between them.
Double check A situation brought about by a discovered check; a piece moves to give check, clearing the way as it does so for another piece to give check at the same time.

Doubled pawns Two or more pawns of the same colour on the same file.

Draw A game that concludes with no player the victor.

Dynamic play Play based on the latent power in the position – usually short lived.

Edge A small advantage.

Elo An international rating system devised by Professor Arpad Elo and used extensively by the International body, FIDE.

En passant See pages 16–17.

En Prise A piece or pawn in a position to be captured.

Endgame The last phase of the game when the opposing Kings begin to take an active part.

Equality A state in which neither sides hold the advantage.

Exchange A means of capturing one piece for another.

Exchange sacrifice Capturing a Knight or a Bishop in exchange for your own Rook.

Family fork A fork that simultaneously attacks a King, Queen and Rook.

Fianchetto The development of a Bishop to g2, g7, b2 or b7 after moving the pawn from the appropriate square to the one in front: either g3, g6, b3 or b6.

FIDE The acronym for *Federation Internationale des Echecs*, the official world governing body of chess.

FIDE Master (FM) The third highest permanent title a player can achieve, gained by reaching an Elo rating of 2300.

Fifty-move rule One of the ways in which a game can be drawn (See page 34.)

File The lines of squares running from White's side to Black's – there are eight files on a chessboard, labelled a to h.

Flank A general term for one side of the board or the other.

Flank opening An opening in which players do not try immediately to occupy the centre with pawns, but rather begin by moving a Knight or one of the fianchetto pawns on g2, g7, b2 or b7.

Forced A move where there is no sensible alternative.

Fork An attack by a piece or pawn on more than one other piece or pawn.

Fortress An endgame position that cannot be broken down by the opposition, in spite of a considerable material advantage.

Fritz One of the most powerful PC-based chess-playing programmes on the market.

Gambit The sacrifice of material, usually a pawn, for some possible advantage; for example, speedier development.

Grandmaster (GM) The highest permanent title available to a player. To attain this title players must achieve certain predetermined scores (norms) in three different events and have an Elo rating of 2500 or above.

Good bishop A Bishop that is unobstructed by pawns and has plenty of free movement around the board.

Half-open file A file on which there are none of your own pawns, but at least one enemy pawn.

Hanging pawns Two pawns of the same colour that stand next to each other on adjacent files but are not supported by other friendly pawns on further adjacent files.

Hole A weakness in the pawn structure inviting the enemy to invade on that square or squares.

Hypermodern A school of thought that believes it is preferable to control the centre from afar rather than occupy it.

Initiative The ability to create threats; in control of the game.

Innovation A new idea in an opening, sometimes referred to as a TN (Theoretical Novelty) in annotation of a game.

International Master (IM) The second highest permanent title available to a player. To attain this title players must achieve certain predetermined scores (norms) in three different tournaments and have a minimum Elo rating of 2400.

Interpose Placing a piece in between an enemy attacker and the piece being attacked.

Isolani An isolated queen pawn (d pawn).

Isolated pawn A pawn on its own with no pawns of its own colour on adjacent files.

Liquidation Process of exchanging several pieces and pawns to clarify a position, often used to prepare for the endgame.

Luft An escape square for the King, preventing the possibility of a back-rank mate.

Major piece A Queen or a Rook.

Mate A shortened, and more commonly used, term for checkmate.

Material A quantity of pieces and pawns.

Mating attack A direct attack against the King with the aim of delivering checkmate.

Middlegame That part of the game encapsulated between the opening and the endgame; the stage where the game begins in earnest.

Minor piece A Bishop or a Knight.

Minority attack An attack by two pawns against three on one of the flanks, usually the Queenside, designed to create weaknesses in the opponent's pawn structure.

Mobility The ability to move pieces freely around the board.

Motif A tactical ploy of some kind.

Multiple fork A fork that simultaneously attacks several pieces at once.

Open A position in which the centre is largely unblocked and pieces can have freedom of movement.

Open file A file unoccupied by pawns.

Open games Openings that begin with the moves 1.e4 e5.

Opening Named sequence of moves at the start of play; for example, the Giucco Piano.

Opposite-coloured bishops A situation where both sides have a Bishop each, both operating on different-coloured squares.

Opposition As well as referring to the person you are playing against, this is a technical term in chess denoting an important ingredient of endgame play where each King opposes the other, along a file, rank or diagonal, with either one, three or five squares between them. The player with the opposition obliges the other King to move first.

Outpost An ideal square for a piece (frequently a Knight) in the enemy's half of the board.

Overload A piece that is overloaded is trying to carry out two or more functions at once.

Overprotection A concept by Aaron Nimzovitch, one of the great Grandmasters of the past, claiming that strategically important points should be protected several times.

Overworked Similar to overloaded.

Passed pawn A pawn that can neither be blocked by an enemy pawn nor captured by one; a pawn fast-tracked for promotion!

Pawn break A pawn move forcing a change in the structure of the position.

Pawn centre The structure of the player's pawns in the middle of the board.

Pawn chain A line of pawns linked together diagonally up the board.

Pawn island A single pawn or a group of connected pawns with no friendly pawns on adjacent files.

Perpetual check A means of checking indefinitely – a drawn position.

Piece A King, Queen, Rook, Bishop or Knight but not a pawn.

Pin A position where a piece cannot move without exposing a more important or unprotected piece to attack. (See pages 34–35.)

Poisoned pawn A pawn that it is not usually advisable to capture.

Positional A style of play based on permanent and semi-permanent features of the game.

Post-mortem Analysis between opponents after the game is over.

Premature A move in a give position undertaken too early.

Preparation This normally refers to finding new ideas in an opening prior to an important game. Top Grandmasters may employ a team of other top players to prepare ideas for them.

Pressure A means of limiting your opponent's possibilities.

Promotion The exchange of a pawn for a piece when it reaches the eighth rank.

Prophylaxis A means of preventing a plan of your opponent's.

Protected passed pawn A 'passed pawn' defended by another pawn on an adjacent file.

Punt Chess slang referring to an ambitious move that hasn't been analysed in any depth.

Queening Promotion of a pawn to a Queen.

Quiet move A move that does not involve a check or capture, but may contain a subtle threat.

Rank A line of squares running across the board.

Refutation Clear demonstration that a plan is unsound.

Resignation A means of conceding the game, traditionally undertaken by laying one's King on its side.

Romantic A swashbuckling style of play popular in the nineteenth century.

Sacrifice An offer of material in the hope of gaining an advantage.

Semi-open game Openings where White begins 1.e4 but Black does not reply 1...e5.

Sharp position A position ripe with tactical possibilities.

Simplification Usually meaning a reduction in material by a series of exchanges.

Skewer Rather like a reverse pin, this is when two pieces are attacked on the same line, with the rear of the two being the intended target. (See pages 36–37.)

Smothered mate A method of checkmate usually delivered by a Knight when the opposition King is unable to move because it is hemmed in by its own army.

Sound A correct move with no weaknesses.

Space A space advantage is where one player or the other has more room in which to manoeuvre successfully.

Spare tempo An important concept in endgame play.

Speculative A move or manoeuvre that has not been thoroughly analysed.

Stalemate A position where the King is not in check but any move it makes causes it to be in check – a drawn game.

Strategy A long-term plan.

Swindle A lucky win or draw.

Symmetry A position where Black has copied White's every move – usually Black is forced to break the symmetry disadvantageously.

Tactics Short-term plans, usually involving pieces in some combinational motif.

Tempo The time needed on the board for a useful move.

Tension Used usually when referring to pawn structures; a situation where either side could either advance pawns or exchange them. Strong players like to maintain the tension for as long as is practicable.

Threefold repetition Another drawing mechanism whereby exactly the same position occurs three times. (See page 33.)

Time control The rate of play set by the organizers of a match or tournament.

Time pressure The point at which players have to move much faster than the average rate set.

Time trouble Acute time pressure.

Transposition A method used to reach the same position via a different move order than usual.

Trap A subtle move, which leads the opponent to think a move is safe, when, in fact, it loses.

Under-promotion Promoting a pawn to anything other than a Queen.

Unsound A move that should not succeed if the opponent plays accurately.

Variation Usually this means a subdivision of a particular opening. For example, the Evans Gambit is a variation of the Giucco Piano.

Weak pawn A pawn that cannot easily be defended or move out of the line of attack.

Weak square A square that is liable to invasion by members of the opposing army.

Weakness Any facet of a position that may be easily exploited by your opponent.

Zugzwang A state of play where a player, on his turn, is obliged to make a weakening move; most common in the endgame.

Zwischenzug An in-between move, such as a check or important threat to the enemy, before recapturing or making what may have seemed like an obligatory move.

INDEX

ACKNOWLEDGEMENTS

Executive editor **Trevor Davies**
Editor **Alice Bowden**
Executive art editor **Karen Sawyer**
Designer **Lisa Tai**
Illustrator **Peter Liddiard**
Production Manager **Ian Paton**